TABLE OF CONTENTS

CW00410438

FOREWORD

EARLY INTERVENTION

RESTORATIVE JUSTICE

DIVERSITY

PROGRAMMES FOR YOUNG OFFENDERS

FOREWORD

The Conference in June 1998 was opened by Mr Henry McLeish, the Minister of State at The Scottish Office with responsibility for Home Affairs, including policy on criminal justice matters. Mr McLeish noted that all the jurisdictions represented at the conference shared common problems with young people and crime although each country was developing approaches to tackling them which respected relevant social and legal frameworks. The children's hearings system added a unique dimension to the approach being developed in Scotland.

Mr McLeish set out two main themes. The first was that the Government was committed to being tough on crime, but was determined to re-define what "tough" meant. Whatever action was taken should be challenging to both offenders and communities. Offenders had to be helped to accept responsibility for their behaviour and criminal behaviour had to be changed through help and support. Communities had to seek to influence the conditions that create delinquency and assist in the process of addressing offending behaviour.

The second theme outlined by the Minister was that the wider picture had to be addressed. Indicators showed that in Scotland one third of children lived in poverty. Forty one per cent of the under 5's lived in families where the money coming in was less than half the average national wage. Poverty was not an excuse for offending behaviour by children and young people. But social exclusion damaged society. The Minister advocated policies of social inclusion, working in partnership between central and local government and the voluntary sector. The children's hearings system and the approach to young people in the criminal justice system must be seen as part of a wider campaign to tackle the conditions which may give rise to crime. Young people had to be enabled to feel part of society, where their self worth and confidence should be a positive dynamic in society.

Mr McLeish spoke about two pilot projects funded by the Government. The first was Freagarrach, run by Barnardos, which sought to confront the most persistent young offenders in Central Scotland through a structured targeted approach with both the children and their families. Internal evaluation pointed to positive results with older age offenders (i.e. 14-16). The other project was that run by Apex (Scotland) in Fife which sought to enhance employment opportunities among young offenders (14-16 year olds). Mr McLeish also noted that alternative approaches should also be considered, such as mediation and reparation schemes.

Since the conference in 1998, there have been several key developments. From 1 July 1999, the Scottish Executive assumed responsibility for criminal justice matters, answerable to the Scottish Parliament. Following the elections, a coalition was formed between the Labour Party and the Scottish Liberal Democrats based on a Partnership Agreement. This provided a new focus for action, with a commitment to direct resources into preventing and reducing re-offending. A post of Minister for Justice was created, currently held by the Deputy First Minister, Mr Jim Wallace. Responsibility for the children's hearings system lies with Mr Sam Galbraith, Minister for Children and Education.

At its first strategy session in November 1999, the Scottish Cabinet met to discuss youth crime. It has begun a review of the range of options available to decision makers, whether in the children's hearings system or the courts, and of their effectiveness. A report will be made back to the Cabinet in early Spring 2000, following consultation with the public and relevant organisations.

A further pilot early intervention scheme for 8–14 year olds has also been established (the Matrix project) with a view to reducing factors leading to risk of offending and enhancing positive influences in their lives. This project draws in all key agencies involved in supporting children and young people and aims to provide support to families as well.

The Scottish Executive has made a start in developing its Social Inclusion agenda and by examining how policy development can be better developed. It looks forward to continuing contact in the years ahead through gathering such as the Standing Conference on Children Young People and Crime.

The Scottish Executive
January 2000

SETTING THE SCENE

Barry Anderson, Chief Executive – Communities That Care (UK)

I have to start with an apology to those of you who were expecting to hear from Jon Bright, who is unfortunately unable to be with us. I shall not attempt to cover the same territory, instead I want to share with you some of the thinking behind this conference.

The event has been jointly organised by a group of just seven people, drawn from seven different agencies - statutory and non-statutory - in four different jurisdictions. I'd like just to thank them, on your behalf, for all their hard work. I want, in particular, to thank

> Monica Barry, of Stirling University who, whilst actively involved in planning the content of the programme, has also shouldered most of the administrative and financial arrangements;

> the University itself, which has shown both patience and generosity as we sought to finalise arrangements,

> Dr. Joe Curran, of The Scottish Office, who has bravely agreed to co-ordinate the editorial task for the twenty or so papers you will hear over the next two days,

> and, of course, our sponsors, NCH Action for Children (Scotland), The Northern Ireland Office and The Scottish Office, without whose generous financial assistance this conference simply would not have been possible.

The thinking behind the conference is simply this: that *throughout* Britain and Ireland there is *real* concern about youth crime and that *within* Britain and Ireland there are four different jurisdictions and four very different systems, for *dealing* with youth crime. Compare, for example, the system of Children's Hearings here in Scotland, with the adversarial court-based process which applies South of the border.
And there are other important differences too-
- in the age of criminal responsibility
- in our respective criminal justice procedures
- in the roles played by the different agencies
- in the sentencing options available to courts (especially in relation to the contentious area of secure and custodial sentencing)

But for all these *differences*, those working in youth justice often find themselves confronting precisely the *same* issues:
- the challenge of change: both legislative and organisational
- the issue of diversity and the challenge to develop anti-discriminatory practice

- the problem of transition: when *should* a young person in trouble enter an adult criminal justice system, devoid of all the safeguards built into our various juvenile procedures?
- the phenomenon of persistent offenders (not to mention their demonisation in the media). What do we *mean* by persistence? And how *should* we respond to young people who offend repeatedly?
- And what do we do about *serious* offenders? Where I come from, there is a worrying tendency to talk about 'serious and persistent offenders' as a single group. The reality, of course, is that some repeat offenders commit relatively minor offences, whilst some of the most serious offences, including rape and murder (though these are mercifully extremely rare offences among juveniles) may well be committed by young people with no previous convictions.

These issues and many others no doubt, are common to all the jurisdictions represented here. Not surprisingly, therefore, our strategies aimed at dealing with these issues also have much in common. I think we probably all share an interest, for example, in:
- effective inter-agency work
- prevention and early intervention
- the techniques of restorative justice

These are just three examples of *important* developments being pursued relatively *independently* by policy-makers and practitioners in all four jurisdictions. The same is true, to a large extent, of our research communities. Recent years have seen a growing interest in research into the risk and protective factors which affect the likelihood of young people becoming involved in crime, and in the programmes which appear to be successful in tackling criminality. In a British context, for example, one thinks of Professor David Farrington's work on 'Understanding and Preventing Youth Crime' and, more recently still, the research review published by The Scottish Office this year, which was based on an exhaustive survey of world literature undertaken by a team of researchers from Glasgow University, led by Professor Stewart Asquith.

So part of the thinking behind today's conference is that we would all benefit from an opportunity to *share* our knowledge, our experience and our research about:
- what works - the outcome of our respective systems
- our common interests - and how we are tackling them
- the lessons we learn, as we develop new ideas

That's why this conference has been designed as a *participative* event, for a multi-disciplinary, invitation-only, *expert* audience. I think we also felt that the *time* was now right for a conference like this. Gerry, in his opening remarks, touched on some of the reasons and the Minister has just delivered an address which illustrates the point perfectly. The increasing emphasis on tackling social exclusion provides both a challenge and an opportunity. First, I believe we are *challenged* to say what an inclusive response to youth crime might look like; not an easy question, but, *again* in putting together the programme for this event we have tried to offer *some* possible answers.

Presumably, an *inclusive* approach prioritises the needs of both victims and young people at risk or in trouble, which again is why we are interested in:
preventing crime wherever possible
early intervention when problems arise
a more *restorative* approach to criminal justice

But the notion of social exclusion also implicitly recognises the complex nature of social disadvantage and the need to address issues such as crime *nationally* (within the context of a broader social policy agenda) and *locally* through a coherent strategy to tackle exclusion (what is sometimes called `joined-up thinking'). As you heard a moment ago, I am involved in a new initiative called Communities that Care (UK). I am not going to say too much about CTC, (our guidebook is in your packs) but it does, I think, illustrate the added dimension which the whole notion of social exclusion brings to our work on youth crime. Communities that Care is an evidence-based programme designed to tackle youth crime, school failure, drug abuse and school-age pregnancy by reducing the risk factors and promoting the protective factors which make it more or less likely that they will develop these problems.

A useful analogy is with coronary heart disease. We know that if we tackle:
- cholesterol
- obesity
- smoking
- excessive drinking
- poor diet
- lack of exercise
- stress

and promote healthier lifestyles, we can reduce the incidence of heart disease in the population. We know too that we will have other benefits, e.g. reducing smoking will reduce the incidence of lung cancer and number of respiratory illnesses. Similarly, a meta-analysis of 50 years research (primarily into youth crime) has helped to identify a number of risk factors which 'drive' the problem of youth crime. I will not go into detail, but can tell you (I am sure that you won't be surprised) that they encompass a range of personal, social and economic factors and that they have much to do with the family, the school and the community environment.

Most important, though, is the fact that of 17 identified risk factors for youth crime, 15 correlate with school failure, 14 correlate with drug abuse and 9 correlate with school-age pregnancy. In other words, as I suspect we have all known for some time, we are dealing with complex, interacting multiple problems, requiring multiple solutions in a single, sophisticated strategy. I think that one of the things which motivated us in organising this conference was the knowledge (each from the viewpoint of our own jurisdiction) that the current debate on social exclusion gives us a real opportunity to develop such coherent strategies and so makes the bringing-together of the 80 strong panel of experts from across Britain and Ireland both more valuable and more urgent.

We hope you like the way the conference programme has been organised. We hope you find the papers stimulating. But most of all, we hope you make use of this opportunity to talk to each other; to renew or perhaps, establish lasting dialogue.

There are 80 specially-invited experts here, and that in itself is a potentially invaluable resource.

Have a good time using it.

OPENING ADDRESS BY GERRY O'HARA, DIRECTOR, NCH ACTION FOR CHILDREN, SCOTLAND

Introduction to Public Policy Agenda

Before raising some key Scottish issues it is appropriate to take a step back, to look more broadly at developing public policy trends in this area.

The first fifteen months of the new Labour Government have been ones of great activity: countless policy reviews have been initiated, Task Forces established and a flurry of consultation papers produced. Some new legislation relevant to children and families is now on the statute book, and more is planned. A clear pattern is beginning to emerge of how this Government is seeking to address the complex social problems facing Britain, whether in the fields of crime, public health or social exclusion.

Some people are calling this approach 'the New Public Management' which is now expressed most clearly within the 'big idea' of Best Value. The emphasis seems to be on tackling problems at local level through a process of auditing needs and existing services, developing strategic responses by means of cross departmental, multi-agency planning exercises, setting objectives and then monitoring and evaluating outcomes to feed back into the 'planning loop'. There is much talk of consumer involvement in all these activities but at present the rhetoric probably outweighs the reality. Most organisations would almost certainly acknowledge that they could be doing more in this respect.

Local Authorities are invariably in the lead in carrying through these initiatives, as indeed they should be. The emphasis is appropriately on the corporate and enabling roles of local authorities: in recognition of the fact that few, if any, social problems can now be solved unless local authority departments work together in partnership with other public services such as the Police, Health Authorities and the voluntary and private sectors.

Although this way of working is challenging and undoubtedly more successful in some places than others, this has to be the right approach, not least because it offers the possibility of much more coherent, integrated and therefore effective responses to addressing social needs. An interesting question yet to be answered however, is how much positive impact 'the New Public Management' will be able to make in the face of continuing public expenditure restrictions. Quality has a cost.

The importance of developing more integrated policy responses has been recognised centrally as well as locally. The most obvious demonstration to date is the establishment of the Social Exclusion Unit in the Cabinet Office. The various Ministerial Groups, e.g. on the Family and on Women, are also attempts to generate a cross Government approach to key policy issues.

Another trend which has become evident during the year is that of devolution. As a result of the majorities achieved in the referenda we now await the establishment of a Scottish Parliament, a Welsh assembly and a London authority. These new institutions (and possibly, in the future, similar ones in the English regions) imply the establishment of significant centres of authority outside of Westminster. There is, therefore, a potential tension between this diversification of influence on the one hand and the desire for policy integration on the other. It will be interesting to see how these two forces play themselves out in the next period.

The Role of the Voluntary Sector and its relationship to government

As a leading children's charity, a key concern for NCH Action For Children is the extent to which the actual and potential contributions of the voluntary sector are being recognised and supported within current social policy initiatives, against a context in which the Prime Minister has called for real partnership between Government, the voluntary sector and others.

There are some encouraging developments to report here. We have for example, been impressed by the way in which the Social Exclusion Unit has energetically engaged with voluntary sector activity on the ground, to feed good practice back into central policy making. We also welcome the initiative of seeking to develop a 'compact' - a formal understanding of roles and responsibilities between Government and the Voluntary Sector.

These are early days in the development of these new relationships and there are many issues yet to be resolved. For example, while Government Consultation papers now routinely include references to the role of voluntary organisations they can sometimes seem tokenistic and the voluntary sector contribution in meeting local needs is often underestimated. Larger agencies like NCH Action For Children are not only major service providers, they are also often uniquely placed to bring other organisations and public services together in the best interests of families and communities. At the other end of the spectrum, smaller voluntary organisations can often engage parts of the community that statutory agencies cannot possibly reach on their own. These very different but equally important roles both need to be recognised and encouraged.

Similarly, the task of negotiating an appropriate relationship between the voluntary sector and government is by no means easy, since this entails tackling difficult issues such as the management of a partnership which is inherently unequal, the imperative for voluntary organisations of retaining 'their voluntaries' and the problem for government of how to engage with the diversity and sheer 'messiness' of the sector.

In our view, a major change for government and the voluntary sector over the next year will be to work together to devise structures which support and encourage voluntary action and involve the sector fully in consultation and in development without destroying the essence of what is so uniquely valuable about the voluntary sector.

Our approach to the twin issues of responding to youth crime and encouraging safety approach

Tackling youth crime is a priority for this government, just as it was for the last. It has often been in the news this year and government has pressed ahead with green and white papers and with draft legislation for England.

Many of the proposals which have been advanced are, at least in part, welcome. In particular, the decision to develop Youth Offending Teams south of the border as part of a more strategic, multi-agency approach to tackling youth crime at local level. As a major provider of community based youth justice services, NCH Action For Children hopes to be engaged in helping in the development of the Teams in different areas of the country, contributing from our existing practice.

In the light of the Adult Commission research showing that too much money invested in tackling youth crime is spent on processing systems and not enough on prevention, it is sincerely hope that the development of youth offending teams will encourage the transfer of resources towards service to engage and divert young offenders and to prevent youth crime. We know that these services do work in reducing offending and encouraging more responsible and engaged attitudes in young people. They are not 'soft options' but are designed to make young people take responsibility for their actions in a way which a mainly punitive response does not encourage.

Several NCH Action For Children projects are piloting family group conferences as a means of challenging young offenders about their offending behaviour and encouraging them to take responsibility for it. More generally, the 'restorative justice' approach is welcome because professional experience suggests that this is effective.

Also welcome is the increased commitment to meeting the needs of victims, many of whom are themselves young people.

Responses to youth crime should be determined first and foremost by an informed understanding of 'what works - in the best interests of the whole community'. Custodial sentences should be avoided wherever possible, since all the evidence suggests that re-offending rates are higher here than with community based responses. None the less, it is acknowledged that for a very small proportion of young offenders we have no current alternative to detention because they are either a risk to themselves or to others. While that is the case and where prison is the only available option, it is imperative that young prisoners are kept separate from adult prisoners, are safe and that their welfare is adequately promoted through education and health.

Home Office research carried out under the last government showed that while in the past, most young men who committed offences 'grew out of it' in their early twenties, this is no longer so often the case. High levels of unemployment prevent young men from settling down in a job and a family. This highlights the importance of creating high quality training places and 'real jobs', especially in disadvantaged areas, as an important part of a crime prevention strategy. We also need to think about how to offer hope and a place in the community to all young people. This is not only about paid work, it is about fatherhood and families.

The renewed emphasis being placed on the importance of supporting families as part of a longer term approach to preventing youth crime is welcomed. However, we would emphasise the need for positive engagement with families as the way forward rather than a top down imposition of rules and penalties. So also is the community safety perspective to combating crime and the fear of crime. Crime prevention schemes in disadvantaged districts should be expanded, in accordance with local priorities, including those of the young people of a community who are often victims of violence, theft, bullying and sexual threat and abuse. These preventive measures might be the 'designing out' of the potential for crime, improving the physical safety of areas by lighting, traffic calming measures and they also should include the upgrading of home security measures.

But whatever else happens, positive steps must be taken to integrate young people - including young offenders - into the initiatives that are developed. If we do not involve young people, there is a risk that they could be further marginalised and excluded, which would be in the best interests of no-one. In this respect, there has to be some concerns that the Curfew Orders contained in the governments proposals for England and Wales may alienate young people from communities, especially if they are policed in an insensitive way. In Scotland, we have the example of the Hamilton Curfew, or Child Protection Initiative, which does, on early evaluation, seem to have caused greater alienation among many of the young people and sometimes their parents or carers.

Tackling Crime In Context

The provision of services to young people who offend cannot be delivered within a vacuum of punishment. In order to be effective, we must address issues that affect behaviour, e.g. poverty, homelessness, education, etc. Criminal Justice service delivery should be effective and innovative and provide the courts and Social Work Departments with credible community based disposals for young people who offend and who are at serious risk of custody, irrespective of race, gender, disability or sexuality.

The objective of Social Work in Scotland, enshrined in the Social Work Scotland Act of 1968, is 'to promote social welfare and social justice through helping to alleviate personal and social problems and seeking to enhance the quality of life of individuals, families and communities'. Social Work is rooted in the belief that the origins of personal and social problems, including criminal behaviour, may not only be found in the exercise of individual choice but also in the factors over which the individual has little or no control.

Promoting effective practice in Criminal Justice Social Work Services

So, what are our aims in providing criminal justice services?

Firstly, to ensure that in particular, community supervision contributes to community safety and offender integration.

Secondly, to increase judicial and public confidence in the quality of the service. Thirdly, to provide best value.

However, we have a long way to go before we can say that we have achieved these three aims. It is true that a tremendous body of knowledge has been acquired over the past 8 years and that this is now the backbone of a 'What Works' approach to providing these services. It is important to identify and promote the application of the knowledge skills and resources which managers and practitioners need in order to provide programmes for supervising offenders in the community. These have to include a recognition that community safety is just as integral to the work as community integration of offenders. Indeed both are sides of the same coin.

Reduction in the use of Custody

Scotland has consistently had a high proportion of people in custody with approximately 21% of its prison population being offenders between 16 and 20 years. In fact, this is the age group most at risk of imprisonment in Scotland. This is despite the most convincing evidence that prison does not work in reducing offending. Even the argument that prisons reduce offending by taking the perpetrators off the street does not hold water in the face of clear evidence that prison educates and qualifies the young person for a life of crime. It also costs more - about five to ten times more - than effective community alternatives.

Appropriate Intervention

Intervention in the lives of young people who offend should be targeted appropriately and practitioners should formulate planned responses proportionate to the seriousness of the offending behaviour. It is important that intervention at too early a stage does not serve to label and to draw the young person into an unnecessary and unhelpful association with other troubled and troublesome young people. It is just as important that serious and clear warning signs that a young person is getting deeper and deeper into offending are acted upon at an early stage. Children's Hearings need to have effective resources available for the under sixteens who are offending. Sixteen is too late and too great a cost for the young person as well as for society.

Community based Supervision

Schemes should directly challenge offending and aim to strengthen and support young people's links with home, the work place and the community and provide a more effective way of engaging serious, persistent offenders rather than the costly and negative experience of custody.

Monitoring and Evaluation

This has to be part of any service offered. The collection of statistical information and the evaluation of that information are central to be able to argue for change. The impact of any changes has to be continuously monitored and adjustments made in policy and practice. It is also important that services are monitored and evaluated in a qualitative way as well as quantitative. It is also important that when we develop and pilot new ways of doing things that these are rigorously evaluated and monitored. We cannot stick only to what works - we need to know what will work better. Only evaluation can tell us that.

Social Exclusion

The experience of social exclusion invariably features in the backgrounds of the young offenders in our Criminal Justice and Children's Hearing projects. Once they have become involved in an offending cycle and quite often have received custodial sentences, they face enormous difficulties in obtaining acceptance in local communities and in securing and retaining employment. An important part of the work of our Criminal Justice projects is therefore not only to help them develop the maturity to take responsibility for their actions but also to offer them realistic, sustainable routes out of offending. This involves building bridges with local communities, many of which are themselves seriously disadvantaged. Strategically, it means ensuring that the needs of these young people are taken into account in the development of community safety plans and regeneration initiatives.

Social exclusion is often geographically distributed, it typically affects people of all ages in the community and because it is a product of the interaction of many social, economic and demographic forces, combating it is a long term (10 year plus) task, requiring sustained attention and funding. There are good reasons for placing special focus on those who are the future of the community because the opportunity for significantly increasing their life chances through making successful interventions is greater than with adults.

Early Intervention

Whilst this conference may focus upon children and young people with offending histories, it is important that we don't lose sight of the fact that support for families in difficulty is a general safety net which helps prevent all sorts of problems developing. Our family centres help socially excluded parents develop the skills and self confidence which they need if they are to access more formal initiatives and in the process to build the capacity of local communities (e.g. through supporting credit union and food co-ops). Parents who are empowered in this way are much more likely to be able to encourage a similar citizenship and participation in their children.

The Present Government View

As already stated, the Labour government does recognise the scale and nature of social problems, although there are many different views about what the solutions might be. Therefore, debate has shifted from demonstrating problems to finding solutions, and government is looking to local authorities and the voluntary sector to help design and implement these but only within the ideological parameters it has set. This can be a frustrating experience for those of us who would challenge some of the assumptions about individuals and society that seem to be behind these parameters.

However, within these constraints, local authorities and voluntary organisations have been granted greater access to central policy making than in the past. Optimistically we can only assume that that this opportunity is also an opportunity to challenge and to jettison any ideological obstacles to the full inclusion of all children and young people in a society which offers them all hope and security.

We look forward to a growing and positive relationship with government and with local authorities in developing policies and services which really make a difference to children, young people and their families.

EARLY INTERVENTION

Superintendent Patrick J. McGowan, An Garda Síochána, Ireland

Introduction

The subject of my paper is early intervention and I will begin with a reference to the maternity hospital which is about as early as I can start. I recall the words of Vincent Brown, one of Ireland's "Media Guru's" at a recent conference on youth matters. He stated that if you walked along a row of cots or incubators in any of Dublin's maternity hospitals and checked the names and addresses of those apparently equal babies you could forecast with a fair degree of accuracy which of those children would complete 3rd level education or, who would by the age of 12 end up on the street, out of school, out of home and out of control. It is a sad indictment of our society when such predictions can be made.

Jim Connolly of Rural Resettlement Ireland points out in his booklet "Quality of Life" that it is extremely difficult, if not impossible, to discuss Irish society in this regard without appearing to be apportioning blame to one section, to be patronising to another and overall to be adapting a holier than thou attitude. However, if we are to succeed, we need to accept the principle that all of us have a shared responsibility for one another. At the present time, the concept of what a community is, needs to be examined. Heather Strang of Canberra University pointed out when speaking on restorative justice that today's communities consist of people we barely know at all. Our real community, the people whom we care most about, consists of the people we work or study with, members of our families spread across the country and friends from many walks of life. When we break the law we may care little for the opinion of those in our geographic community and so experience little shame for the offence. Unfortunately the "I'm alright Jack" syndrome operates across all of our communities and lack of care for others is not just a feature of marginalised communities. In fact there sometimes can be greater mutual co-operation in poverty stricken areas than among the middle and upper classes.

Regarding the identity of communities we learned a little of this in Dublin in 1996, when we introduced our anti-drugs initiative – "Dochas" which in the Irish language means hope. Within inner city communities we found that the occupants of one block of apartments felt that they were a totally distinct community to the one across the street. We would have made the mistake of lumping them all together as one group until the consultative process revealed otherwise. The fact that the Assistant Commissioner took a hands on interest in them and introduced a "Personal Garda" to them, proved to be very useful and went along way towards building trust and mutual co-operation.

Garda Initiatives

With regard to early intervention, I intend to share with you some of our experiences, initiatives and projects which involve the Garda Síochána with the local community.

The various issues which I will cover are:

- The Garda Schools Programme
- Juvenile Diversion Programme
- Community Policing
- Special Garda Projects
- Youth Achievement Awards
- Orienteering for Life
- Copping On

Schools Programme

Up to 1,500 Gardaí have been trained in presentation skills to prepare them for going into primary schools. Research indicated that children in 5th class, i.e. for 10-11 year olds, were the most suitable to receive the benefits of such intervention. 5 visits per year are made between September and June and deal with the areas of:

- The role of the Garda
- Personal safety
- Road safety
- Vandalism
- Bullying
- Drugs

A recent study by the area partnership in North Clondalkin, indicated that intervention was needed at second class or about age 7. That report indicated that in second class children were happy in school, with their teacher and all their subjects, even the less popular subjects. By 5th class they had a 25% absenteeism rate. It was also found that many children were unable to make the transition from primary to secondary school as they were unable to cope with up to 8 teachers and classrooms. Parents were afraid to come to school to address issues as their experience regarding schools was to be called in to deal with some problem in relation to their child. A pilot scheme which covered only 4 basic subjects brought attendance levels up to 100%. Home school liaison teachers and parent support groups including homework groups has done much to improve the situation. However, there is still a great deal of illiteracy among young people. The Department of Education is currently introducing a new initiative in this regard.

Our schools programme has the support of the Irish National Schools Organisation and the Department of Education. A study of the effects of the programme, was recently carried out by Garda Naoimi De Rís of the Garda Schools Programme Office. Her findings were that across the board among all socio-economic groups there was a major improvement in attitude towards and knowledge of the Gardaí among the children who had participated in the programme as against those who did not.

Juvenile Liaison Diversion Programme

Juvenile Liaison in Dublin was set up in 1963. It was extended country wide in 1981. In 1991 a National Juvenile Office was established. A team of 1 Superintendent, 1 Inspector, 9 Sergeants and 82 Gardaí work within it on a national basis. Last year over 13,000 young people were referred to the scheme. One of the advantages of having a national office is that it provides consistency in relation to juvenile justice around the country. It prevents the scenario of juvenile justice by geographical location depending on the whim of a particular District Officer. Where there is any question of a prosecution of a young person under 18 years of age that decision is made by the Director or in a limited number of cases by the Director of Public Prosecutions. All cases involving juveniles are referred to the National Juvenile Office, those involving informal and formal caution and those for prosecution. The diversion programme is being included in total in the new Children Bill. This is perhaps a reflection of the success of the programme to date. An interesting new development in the Restorative Justice field is that Family Conferencing is included in the Bill. Garda Juvenile Liaison officers are nominated as facilitators.

Community Policing

Often new initiatives have their beginnings in disasters or serious incidents. Such was the case with the establishment of community policing in the urban sprawl of Tallaght in South West Dublin in 1988. I had the personal experience of being an outdoor uniformed Inspector on a Sunday afternoon when the body of a young 14 year old murder victim was found in a local park. All gates to the park were locked and until keys were obtained to gain entrance, patrol cars were left outside while we went on foot to preserve the scene. All patrol cars were damaged extensively and a large group of hostile youths made the scene preservation very difficult.

This occurrence was very disturbing – even though we were there investigating the death of one of their neighbours their animosity was palpable. It was a reflection of relationships at the time as policing methods then were reactive. Resulting from this incident which caused major media attention a report on the area was prepared and highlighted all the relevant factors in the area such as, unemployment, poor public transport, single parent families, drug abuse etc. This report resulted in the beginning of community policing for Tallaght whose population had risen from 10,000 to 80,000 between 1970 and 1988 with little support services for the people living there. The strength of the team now stands at 1 Inspector, 2 Sergeants and 28 Gardaí who work full time on foot among the communities where they know and are known to the people. Similar type policing has now spread across all divisions in the city of Dublin.

Special Projects

In 1991 in the Ronanstown area, following riots which resulted in the serious injury of a young child by a petrol bomb, the first Department of Justice, funded Special Garda Projects were set up. From this emerged "Give Ronanstown a future today", or GRAFT as it is commonly known, costing in the region of £70,000 pounds per annum i.e. the cost of keeping one young person in custody for a year. A full time project co –ordinator is employed and the project is community-based, involving multi-agency input from the local community, probation welfare service, youth organisations and the Gardaí. An evaluation study of the usefulness of these projects is currently being prepared. A further study is being carried out to examine if there was real involvement by the people from within the community and to ensure that this wasn't just an exercise of doing things to people rather than with them and for them.

As a result of our direct involvement with these projects we learned that:

- Projects must be community based with a strong community involvement. Community volunteers should if possible be involved in the design stage of the project. This increased their appreciation of the aims and installs a sense of ownership.
- Training for all personnel involved in the project should be provided. It is essential that all persons involved be skilled in dealing with young people. The desired attributes should include good communication and social skills, the ability to deal with groups, to detect behavioural change and resolve conflict.
- It is essential to link with the other related services in the catchment area. This approach serves to compliment effort and to maximise resources.

Garda Youth Achievements Awards

This is a new initiative which was started in West Cork three years ago. The scheme is sponsored by local business interests. Nominations are invited from various organisations involved with youth including schools. Nominations are put forward in respect of young people who have contributed in some way to society in their locality. It gives something back to these young people who are doing worthwhile work and it is a change to the normal criticism which tends to be levelled towards youth in general. At the presentation of awards up to 300 people attend with much positive publicity in the area and spin off benefits for Garda community relations. The scheme is now operating in 3 Garda Divisions and we are extending it to the rest of the country.

Orienteering for Life

A recent initiative begun by a Juvenile Liaison Officer in the Irishtown area of Dublin has had some degree of success. The idea is to apply the concept of orienteering to life. It is aimed at 11 and 12 year old children, small groups of whom are brought to the Dublin mountains for a day accompanied by their teacher and juvenile liaison officer. The orienteering test is built around 11 questions dealing with drug abuse, crime, alcohol abuse and personal safety. We are currently working on the extension of this scheme to the areas worst affected by drugs in Dublin city. Resources have been made available to further develop this scheme.

Copping On

Another multi-agency initiative developed with the Department of Education and Science and the Department of Justice, Equality and Law Reform is the implementation of a national crime awareness programme within youth reach which is facilitated by Youthreach Staff, Garda Juvenile Liaison officers, Youth workers and related agencies.

Apart from getting young people at risk to look at their behaviour in a constructive way, it enables various organisations to examine ways of building co-operation on various issues and to draw up joint programmes.

Conclusion

I have focussed this paper to concentrate on problems associated with young people and crime. I realise that Garda efforts and the new Juvenile Justice Legislation is just one small piece of a larger jigsaw of both statutory and non-statutory initiatives and responses, in trying to deal with children at risk. We would regard non attendance at school as probably the main specific early indicator that a child is on the slippery slope towards a life of crime and vandalism. To succeed a co-ordinated approval is necessary. At present a feasibility study is being carried out between South and East Belfast Trust, Dublin and Torku in Finland, involving interested agencies in all 3 locations to establish ways of identifying young people at risk. This initiative is known as Sharing Information on Troubled Young Adults.

The appointment of a Junior Minister to deal with children's affairs across various government departments is a useful development. I am currently on a cross departmental committee examining submissions for projects which are under the auspices of the Department for Health and are being delivered by Barnardos. They are targeting families at risk in a holistic way. Funding is forthcoming on the basis that full and broad consultation takes place with all parties.

Support in Ireland at all levels for helping to prevent juvenile crime is strong and public opinion is fairly sympathetic to the concept of assisting young offenders, rather than applying the full rigours of the law to them. There is still much public goodwill towards efforts to help children at risk and child offenders.

If I were to make only one important point here over these three days of information sharing it would be the need. It is important that people are treated with respect and are empowered to realise their potential.

EARLY INTERVENTION IN THE SCOTTISH CHILDREN'S HEARINGS

Professor Christine Hallett, University of Stirling, Scotland

---

Early intervention in the Scottish Children's Hearings System

This paper begins with a brief description of the Scottish Children's Hearings System before going on to discuss its potential for early intervention and non-intervention in respect of children and young people who are alleged to have committed offences.

The Children's Hearings System came into operation in Scotland in 1971, implementing in large measure the reform proposals outlined in the Kilbrandon Report (Children and Young Persons Scotland), published in 1964. The system was originally founded on the Social Work Scotland Act, 1968. Although Scots child care law was radically reformed in the Children (Scotland) Act 1995, it is striking that the Children's Hearings System remained largely unchanged in its overall functioning - a testimony to its widespread support. The parts of the 1995 Act most relevant to the Children's Hearings System were implemented in April 1997.

Two key innovations underpinned the system, namely the reporter to the children's panel and the children's hearing itself.

The Reporter to the Children's Panel

The reporter was originally appointed as an official within local government to receive referrals concerning children and young people in difficulty. Since 1996 reporters have been appointed by the Scottish Children's Reporter Administration (SCRA) which operates the reporters service on a national basis as a non-departmental public body. Anyone may refer a child (in Scot's law someone under the age of sixteen) to a reporter, but in practice referrals come predominantly from the police. A key task of the reporter (who usually comes from a legal or social work background) is to determine the initial action to be taken upon receipt of referrals. The main courses of action open to the reporter on receipt of a referral are:

- to decide under S56(4) of the Children (Scotland) Act 1995 that a Children's hearing 'does not require to be arranged'. If that is the case, the child, 'parent' (now known as a relevant person) and the referrer are to be notified of the decision - this is colloquially referred to as 'no further action'.
- the reporter may also, having decided that a children's hearing is not required, refer the case to a local authority (in practice to the social work department) 'with a view to their making arrangements for the advice, guidance and assistance of the child and his (sic) family.' - this is colloquially known as referring for 'voluntary supervision', or for 'advice and guidance'. The options of 'no further action' and 'voluntary supervision' available under S56(4) offer opportunities for early intervention.

The other main option available to the reporter, where it appears 'that compulsory measures of supervision are necessary in respect of the child' is to 'arrange a children's hearing' (S56(6)).

The Children's Hearing

The children's hearing is a lay tribunal of three panel members. The Kilbrandon Report suggested the aim of the hearing would be 'evoking in turn from the parties concerned a constructive response, based on an increased awareness and understanding of their underlying problems and responsibilities' (1964: para 86). At the children's hearing, three panel members, with at least one male and one female member, and a reporter are always present plus, usually, the child or young person, at least one parent or carer and a social worker. Less frequently others such as teachers, family representatives and safe-guarders also attend. Within the context of the hearing, the reporter 'acts in some quasi-legal advisory role' (Finlayson, 1976) and no longer holds the central decision making position as he/she does at the initial investigation stage. The children's hearing has essentially two main options:

- to discharge the referral (S69(12))
- to make a supervision requirement (S70)

Another interim course of action for the hearing members is to continue the case to a subsequent hearing where they are satisfied that further investigation is necessary (S69(2)).

A supervision requirement is made where the Children's Hearing is satisfied that compulsory measures of supervision are necessary (S70(1))

Fundamental Principles of the Children's Hearing System

The Children's Hearings System is founded on several fundamental principles. A key principle of the system is that measures to promote the welfare and best interests of children should be taken within a unified system of justice and welfare based on 'needs' rather than (or as well as) 'deeds'. This follows from the view in the Kilbrandon Report that behaviour such as offending was generally indicative of a failure in upbringing and that measures of 'social education' (para 140) or of 'training appropriate to the child's needs' (para 72) were required. The result was an integrated system (the Children's Hearings System) for dealing with children in difficulty, whether they were referred for reasons of allegedly committing offences, for non-attendance at school or as victims of neglect or ill-treatment. The 'troubled' and the 'troublesome', the 'depraved' and the 'deprived' were to be treated in accordance with a perception of their need for help and pursuit of their best interests.

A second principle is that cases should be heard by lay tribunals, comprising representatives of local communities, in a non-adversarial and relatively informal setting. A further key principle is that there should be an opportunity for children and their parents to participate in discussion both of the nature of the difficulties they were facing and in framing proposed solutions. A fourth principle of the system is the separation of responsibility for deciding on disposals, which is undertaken by the children's hearing, from the determination of the facts (including guilt or innocence), which is adjudicated by the judicial process. If, on appearing before a children's hearing, the grounds of referral are denied, it is open to the panel either to discharge the case or to refer it to the sheriff for adjudication. The standard of proof required before the Sheriff for offence grounds is the criminal one of beyond reasonable doubt. If the sheriff findings the grounds proven, the case is returned to the children's hearing for consideration and disposal. Thirteen per cent of cases referred to hearings on offence grounds in 1995 were remitted to the Sheriff Court for proof (compared with 48% on non-offence grounds).

Opportunities for Early Intervention

The system offers the potential for early intervention at two key points: in reporters' initial decision making and in children's hearings themselves.

Referrals to the Children's Hearing System

The largest source of referrals to the reporter is the police, responsible for 73% of all referrals in 1995. While the rate of referral of children and young people who are alleged to have committed offences fluctuates, somewhat from year to year, the rate is relatively stable; it was 14.4.% of population under 16 in 1985 and 14.0% in 1995.

The age distribution is shown in Table One.
(Insert Figure 1 about here)

The peak age for referral for offending is 15 but referrals for offending begin at age 8, which is the age of criminal responsibility in Scotland and is low by international standards. While the rate of reporting per 1000 population under 16 has remained fairly constant, the number of offences has risen (up by 7% between 1994 and 1995).

(Insert Table 1 about here)
The average number of referrals per child was 2.82%, with a peak of 3.22 at age 14. Of all alleged offence grounds of referral in 1995 (Statistical Bulletin 1997:12), 69% were in respect of boys and 32% in respect of girls (Statistical Bulletin 1997:a).

Reporters' Initial Decision Making

The reporter has two key tasks at the initial stage in appraising a referral:

- to assess the sufficiency of evidence and
- to decide whether compulsory measures of supervision are necessary

If a case is to be referred to a hearing the reporter must establish that there is sufficient evidence to satisfy one of the conditions (or grounds) specified in the Act. Since the system is a unified one, the twelve grounds of referral are wide-ranging, (See Annex 1).

At this point in the reporters' decision-making there is scope for early intervention and for diversion from the children's hearings.

The initial action taken by reporters on referrals in 1995 is shown in Table 2.

(Insert Table 2 about here)

The 61% of offence referrals receiving no further action deserve scrutiny and are detailed in Table 3.

(Insert Table 3 about here)

For the 19% already on supervision, intervention (of some kind) is in place. In respect of the 36% for whom compulsory 'care' (supervision) was deemed unnecessary, other scope for early intervention occurs.

In reaching decisions at this stage, reporters will usually seek reports from schools and social work departments and may have available comments on the referral from the police about, for example, the response of the child and his/her family to apprehension. The reporter will also notify the child and family of the referral and may elicit comments from them. On the basis of these the reporter may decide to take no further action in the light of the nature of the referral and information received. The reporter can also interview the child and parent(s) at this stage and/or make suggestions as to appropriate actions - for example arranging for a young person with a charge of fire raising to spend a day with the fire brigade to help appreciate the consequences of such behaviour.

The 'early intervention' at this stage may rest largely with the parents and/or the child. The fact that the matter has been referred to the reporter and the consequent 'warning shot across the bows' may alert them to take action to avoid further offending. The reporter may also indicate that while no further action has been taken on this occasions, a different view might be taken of any reoccurrence. (Hallet et al, 1998) The fact that reporters are aware that they will be notified if there are further incidents may encourage them in the early stages to take a low key and minimal interventionist approach (consistent with the child's welfare and with the Children (Scotland) Act 1995) (Kuenssberg, 1997:27). Finally it should be noted that a 'no further action' decision signifies that there is no need for compulsory measures, rather than that nothing is being done. The reporter may be satisfied that action is already being taken to meet the child's needs (Kuenssberg, 1997:76).

A second option available is to refer the case to the local authority for advice, guidance and assistance, which occurred in 6 percent of all offence referrals in 1995. Again this offers an opportunity for help to be made available to the family at an early stage and on a voluntary basis.

A third (little need option) is to refer the case back to the police/juvenile liaison officer for a senior police officers' warning. This was used in only two per cent of offence referrals in 1995. It appears that there is variation across the country in the arrangements for these (Kuenssberg, 1997) and also that police warnings are used less frequently in Scotland than in some other jurisdictions.

The Children's Hearing

The last opportunity for early intervention is the children's hearing itself. The Children's Hearing System was founded upon diversion of children and young people from the judicial arena to a lay tribunal. In the intervening years, there has also been a trend towards diversion from hearings themselves, evidenced in the decline in the preparation of referrals from the reporter to hearings. These have fallen from 53 per cent in 1978 to 32 per cent in 1995 (Martin, Fox and Murray, 1981:39, Statistical Bulletin, 1997:13).

Nonetheless, a hearing can provide an opportunity for early intervention (or non-intervention). It is open to the hearing to discharge the case. As is shown in Table 4. In 1995 this occurred in 43% of hearings on offence grounds in respect of boys and girls not already under supervision.

(Insert Table 4 here)
Norrie has noted that:
    'There are many circumstances in which it might be considered appropriate to discharge a referral. The discussion of when the grounds are being considered might have indicated to the members of the hearing that the event which led to the referral (e.g. an incident of petty theft) is unlikely to be repeated......or the hearing may consider that the grounds are simply not serious enough to raise any real concerns for the welfare of the child, or that compulsory measures of supervision simply have nothing to offer the particular child (Norrie, 1997: 110-111).

Slightly more frequently, however, the decision made is to impose a supervision requirement; a decision reached in 56% of hearings in respect of boys not under supervision and 57% of such girls in 1995. (Statistical Bulletin 1997: 17&18).

It is perhaps important to note in passing, however, that the majority of disposals made by children's hearings in 1995 concerned children and young people already under supervision (57% of boys were in this category and 58% of girls), confirming that, on offence grounds, children's hearings are generally (but not always) reserved for a later stage of intervention, (Statistical Bulletin 1997: 17&18) at a point when other 'lighter touch' responses have been deemed to have failed.

Timely Intervention

A variant on 'early' intervention is timely intervention. Time scales for intervention in juvenile justice have received considerable attention recently, for example, in the USA and notably south of the border in the Audit Commission Report (1996)

Misspent Youth, Young People and Crime. They have also received attention in Scotland, for example in the Association for the study of Delinquency Report (1986) Speedy Justice for Children, the Child Care Law Review (1990) and, more recently, in Just in Time (Kuenssberg, 1997).

Table 5 based on unpublished data on time intervals prepared by the Scottish Office shows the time intervals at the four key stages of case processing in respect of children referred on offence grounds.

(Insert Table 5 here)

Since the majority (61%) of referrals on offence grounds are not referred to a hearing, most are dealt with in an average of 111 days (about 3½ months). For those going to a hearing the average was 147 days (just under 5 months). Forty two per cent of offence referrals are dealt with by the reporter in 30 days or less. There is agreement in the Just in Time report that these timescales could and should be shortened, notably by speedier notification from the police, (taking on average 55 days,) by speedier production of reports to the reporters, e.g. from social work departments and schools, and by the minimisation of delays in reporters offices.

In conclusion

The Children's Hearings System offers the potential, and indeed the actuality, for early intervention. It enables the early identification of childrens' needs and problems and the arrangements of prompt intervention through families themselves and through the statutory and voluntary sectors. In so doing, the Children's Hearings System seeks to work in partnership with parents and children. It offers a highly individualised assessment of need, based on the input of a variety of agencies (although the resources identified as necessary are not always secured). It offers the possibility that three young people accused of an identical crime, for example, a minor breach of the peace, may receive very different outcomes. No further action may be taken in respect of one, the second may be referred to the social work department for advice and guidance on a voluntary basis and the third may be referred to a hearing, with the possibility of residential supervision if major needs are identified in the process. The system thus offers, as welfare systems do, the potential for individualised attention but without the strict proportionality associated with more formalised and exclusively justice based jurisdictions.

References

Audit Commission (1996) *Misspent Youth: Young People and Crime*, London: HMSO.

Hallett, C and Hazel N. (1998) *The Children's Hearings System in Context : A Review of Trends in Juvenile Justice and Childcare and Protection Systems,* Edinburgh: Scottish Office Central Research Unit.

Hallett, C., Murray, C. with Jamieson, J. & Veitch, B. (1998) *Decision making in the Scottish Children's Hearings System* Edinburgh: Central Research Unit.

The Kilbrandon Report (1964) *Children and Young Persons Scotland*, Edinburgh: HMSO.

Norrie, K. (1997) *Children's Hearings in Scotland*, Edinburgh: W. Green/Sweet and Maxwell.

Kuenssberg, S. (1997) *Just in Time: Report on Time Intervals in Children's Hearings Cases,* Stirling, Scottish Children's Reporter Administration.

Scottish Office (1999) *Review of Child Care Law in Scotland*, Edinburgh: HMSO.

Statistical Bulletin (1997) *Referrals of Children to Reporters and Children's Hearings 1995-6*, NO SWK/CH/1997/20, Edinburgh: The Scottish Office.

Waterhouse, L., Whyte, B. & McGhee, J. (forthcoming 1999) *Cohort Study: Children's Hearings System,* Edinburgh: Central Research Unit, Scottish Office.

Annex 1: Children (Scotland) Act 1995: grounds of referral

s.52 (1) The question of whether compulsory measures of supervision are necessary in respect of a child arises if at least one of the conditions mentioned in subsection (2) below is satisfied with respect to him.

(2) The conditions referred to in subsection (1) above are that the child
  (a) is beyond the control of any relevant person;
  (b) is falling into bad associations or is exposed to moral danger;
  (c) is likely -
  (i) to suffer unnecessarily: or
  (ii) be impaired seriously in his health or development, due to a lack of parental care;
  (d) is a child in respect of whom any of the offences mentioned in Schedule 1 of the Criminal Procedure (Scotland) Act 1975 (offences against children to which special provisions apply) has been committed;
  (e) is, or is likely to become, a member of the same household as a child in respect of any of the offences referred to in paragraph (d) above has been committed;
  (f) is, or is likely to become, a member of the same household as a person who has committed any of the offences referred in paragraph (d) above;
  (g) is, or is likely to become a member of the same household as a person in respect of whom an offence under sections 2A to 2C of the Sexual Offences (Scotland) Act 1976 (incest and intercourse with a child by step-parent or person in position of trust) has been committed by a member of that household;
  (h) has failed to attend school regularly without reasonable excuse;
  (i) has committed an offence;
  (j) has misused alcohol or any drug, whether or not a controlled drug within the meaning of the Misuse of Drugs Act 1971;
  (k) has misused a volatile substance by deliberately inhaling its vapour, other than for medicinal purposes;
  (l) is being provided with accommodation by a local authority under section 25, or is the subject of a parental responsibilities order obtained under section 86, of this Act and, in either case, his behaviour is such that special measures are necessary for his adequate supervision in his interest or the interest of others.

Table 1: The age of criminal responsibility in Europe, 1995

Country	Age	Country	Age
Andorra	16	Luxembourg	18
Austria	14	Malta	9
Belgium	18	Netherlands	12
Bulgaria	14	Norway	15
Cyprus	7	Poland	16
Czech Republic	15	Portugal	16
Denmark	15	Romania	14
Estonia	15	San Marino	12
Finland	15	Slovakia	15
France	13	Slovenia	14
Germany	14	Spain	16
Greece	12	Sweden	15
Hungary	14	Switzerland	7
Iceland	15	Turkey	12
Ireland	7	United Kingdom:	
Italy	14	England	10
Latvia	14	Wales	10
Liechtenstein	7	Scotland	8
Lithuania	14	Northern Ireland	8

(Source: Council of Europe in Howard League Report, 1995:14)

Figure 1: Age Distribution of Children Referred to Reporters, 1995

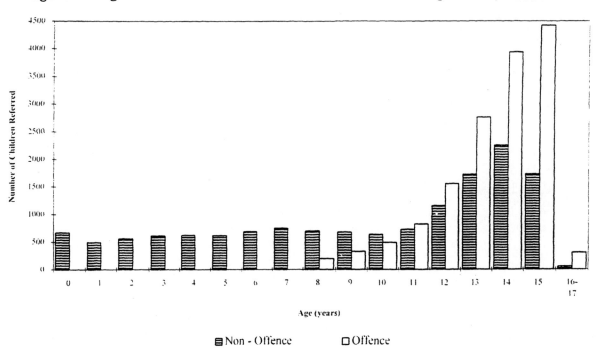

Source: Statistical Bulletin (1997:6)

Table 2:   **Reporters' initial decisions in response to referrals, 1995**

	Percentage All referrals	Offence referrals
No further action 1995	56	61
Referral to:		
SWD/advice and guidance	10	6
Police/juvenile liaison officer	2	2
Children's hearing	32	30

Source: Statistical Bulletin (1997:13)

Table 3: Reason for no further action on grounds referred, 1995

	% of all referrals	% of offence referrals
Under current supervision	15	19
Insufficient evidence	6 (7)[1]	4
Compulsory 'care' unncessary	33	36
Action on other grounds	2	1
	56	61

Source: Statistical Bulletin (1997:13)

---

[1] There is ambiguity about this figure. A blank appears in the relevant table (Table 7: p13) but the text (para 5.1) gives a figure of seven percent.

Table 4: Disposals by hearings on offence grounds 1995:
Children not under supervision

	Boys	Girls
Case discharged	43	43
Supervision requirement made	56	57
Other	1	-

Source: Statistical Bulletin (1997: 17 and 18)

Table 5: Time intervals 1995: offence referrals

Stage 1: incident to receipt of referral by reporter

less than or equal to 30 days   35%
31 to 90 days   52%
90 to 180 days 11%
over 180 days 2%

Average no. of days   55

Stage 2: receipt of referral to reporter's decision

less than or equal to 30 days   42%
31 to 90 days   38%
91 to 180 days 17%
over 180 days 4%

Average no. of days   56

Stage 3: reporter's decision to initial hearing

Less than or equal to 14 days 32%
15 to 30 days   38%
31 to 60 days   21%
over 60 days   9%

Average no. of days   30

Stage 4: initial hearing to disposal

Same day   62%
1-14 days   2%
15-30 days   9%
31 to 60 days   11%
over 60 days   17%

Average no. of days   25

Source: Unpublished data, Scottish Office

RESTORATIVE JUSTICE: ISSUES OF DEFINITION AND EFFECTIVENESS - THE VICTIM'S PERSPECTIVE

David McKenna, Assistant Director (Operations), Victim Support Scotland, Scotland

---

Introduction

The following paper sets out some of the key issues for victims of crime which Victim Support Scotland believes require to be taken into consideration in arriving at any broad definition of restorative justice and ensuring its effectiveness in delivering inclusion, not just for youth, but also for victims of crime and for our communities as a whole.

The Victim as Citizen and Consumer

Standing back for a moment from the various roles of victims, offenders and criminal justice workers, we might want to consider some of the continuing changes in our society which may be worth while bearing in mind while approaching broad issues of criminal justice.

- Today our citizens may be more informed and able to communicate widely. Citizens are much more consumers and as such are less concerned that due process has been done and the rules carried out, than they are about positive outcomes. Today the public wants tangible results.

- The victim, once long forgotten, now has a voice and an identity and their expectations are growing rapidly and ahead of all our present abilities to meet their demands.

- The media has, and will continue to have, a high profile in voicing and amplifying the concerns of our citizens and the demands and expectations of the victim. Politicians are not immune to the media.

There are four independent Victim Support organisations that provide support to victims of crime throughout the UK and Ireland. Operating from more than 500 local bases, around 20,000 volunteers provide help and support to, in the region of, half a million crime victims each year. Yes, pro victim, but no, Victim Support is not anti-offender. Victim Support believes that victims and offenders have needs and rights and are entitled to care and support. We have been pleased to support and work in partnership with a range of initiatives, such as mediation and reparation.

In considering the merits of restorative justice and in particular for our youth, Victim Support is aware not only that many young people between the ages of 12 and 25 commit disproportionate levels of crime, but also that many more young people are themselves victims of crime. Today's victim is very probably tomorrow's offender and vice versa. Our whole society, all of our communities, suffers pain, loss and distress as a result of youth crime.

The Victim's Lot is not a Happy One!

Young offenders may feel excluded, unsupported and misunderstood, let down by society and by the criminal justice system. They are not alone - many victims also feel let down and excluded:

- they have no rights in the criminal justice system, other than as witnesses

- they are not represented in court

- the criminal justice process is not explained to them

- they are not routinely informed as their case progresses

- they have no say in the decision whether and for what to prosecute

- they are rarely awarded compensation by the court

- their case can carry on for sometimes a year or more

- they are often cited at the last minute, causing much distress

- postponements and adjournments can mean up to four or more visits to court by victims

- after all this, the accuse may change his plea and the victim is never called to give evidence

- pleas in mitigation impugning the reputation or attacking the character of the victim often go unchallenged in court, but are widely reported in the press

- throughout this criminal justice process, victims and their families are often subject to attacks, threats, intimidation and harassment which continue well after the case is disposed of

When offences are dealt with by the Children's Panel or a police caution, some of the distress accompanying a court case can be avoided, though the victim remains uninformed, not consulted, not represented, not involved - still excluded. The distress, the threats, harassment, intimidation and fear are often all the more real and can be devastating on the victim's life.

Restorative Justice: Good for the Victim, Good for the Offender and Good for the Community

For many offences, and in particular those often associated with youth crime, community justice as opposed to criminal justice can afford the victim the real opportunity to participate fully in the delivery of a form of justice which is fair and inclusive of all. To be meaningful and genuine, community justice programmes must not be designed nor driven with the interests of either the victim or the offender more at the centre than the other. Such initiatives must formally recognise and balance the needs, rights and interests of victims and offenders from the outset.

The value of restorative justice to the victim of crime is relatively straightforward and understandable in that it provides an opportunity for explanation, reassurance and resolution of the offences. Victims want to know:

- why me?
- that it's not going to happen again
- that the offender knows the impact the crime has had
- what the offender proposes to do to make the harm done

In the formal criminal justice system, none of these primary needs of victims are met. Surprisingly, many victims do not want the offender to have a criminal record or to have to go to court and even in some serious cases, they don't want the offender to go to prison.

There has been extensive research, particularly in the United States, some in the UK, with regard to the value and effectiveness of restorative forms of justice. While there are varying outcomes and differing statistics, I think it's safe to say that we know that not everyone offered the opportunity, both victims and offenders, to participate in community justice will take up the offer. It's probably fair to say that up to a quarter of offenders decide not to participate, with a similar level of victims declining. Yet of both offenders and victims who do take part, towards 90% view the process and the outcome as a positive experience.

But what about the cases that do not proceed - potentially up to 50%? In considering issues of definition and effectiveness of restorative justice, we must also consider the principles and practice which support and promote high levels of participation by all.

There are many tools through which restorative justice can be achieved, including reparation, mediation, compensation and reconciliation. There are many crimes which lend themselves well to restorative justice, including vandalism, damage to property, theft, harassment and in some cases assault and housebreaking.

Some Ground Rules and Principles

I want to briefly set out, from the victim's perspective, key areas of expectation and by doing so, a range of principles which should inform any restorative justice service.

Firstly, some general ground rules:
- Participation in community justice, by both victims and offenders, must be completely voluntary and systems should be designed to militate against any intentional or unintentional coercion of victims or offenders to take part.

- Both victims and offenders must be provided with independent information about the value, purpose, process and explanations which underpin participation.

- Victims and offenders should be provided with independent practical and emotional support throughout their participation in the process.

Secondly, some principles upon which community justice should be based and in setting these out I have drawn heavily on the paradigms of justice set out by Zehr in 1990 (Zehr, H (1990) Changing Lenses, Scottdale, PA: Herald).

Community Justice should require:
- the direct involvement of both victims and offenders
- recognition of the rights of victims and the responsibility of offenders
- the stigma of the offence should be removable, through the offender recognising the impact of the crime, taking responsibility for it and making amends
- the community rather than the state should be the facilitator of justice
- crime should be seen more as a violation of one person by another and less as a violation of the state
- reconciliation and restoration should be objective, not punishment
- justice should be more about successful outcomes than the process having been gone through and the rules followed
- it should be more important to establish dialogue and negotiation than to be adversarial
- less attention should be focused on what happened in the past and more on solving the problem for the future

There are also a number of fundamental questions which require consideration, discussion and agreement:

- What about the victim's right to request that a crime should be dealt with within the community and not the formal criminal justice system

- Should not any system of restorative justice give the right to both victim and offender to positively request access to community justice?

- What is the role of the prosecution service in determining who and which crimes should get access to community justice? Should the prosecution have a role?

- How do we ensure national standards of service; ensure that no matter where you live as victim or offender you have the same rights of access to the same services?

- Which agency, government, statutory or voluntary, should be responsible for the management and delivery of community justice? Should there not be a new independent agency charged with this responsibility?

Some tough questions but ones which nonetheless need to be considered.

In Conclusion

So, almost in conclusion, can I say that Victim Support recognises the role restorative justice can play in making our communities safer. We are willing and well placed nationally and locally to play a part, in partnership, to secure a new way forward for justice in our communities. We will work with government and others to secure positive change.

Finally, we all care about victims, offenders, our communities, our people. Together, with the tremendous amount of commitment, enthusiasm, knowledge and experience we all have, we can change the future for the better and we will.

RESTORATIVE JUSTICE IN IRELAND

Dr. Valerie Bresnihan, Chairperson, Irish Penal Reform Trust

Introduction

When we think of crime and its solutions we are culturally conditioned to think of prisons. Prisons are symbolically powerful and the idea of retribution is far more impressive than its poor relation, reparation, something of which I hope to talk about today. Regrettably, Irish prisons are no exception to this cultural association. Recently, Mountjoy Prison Visiting Committee took the unusual step of re-submitting their previous annual report (1996) as an attempt both to draw attention to the appalling conditions in the largest prison in the country and, in particular, to focus on the political apathy that surrounds our prison system, a system that has little or no rehabilitative programmes, no sense of planning and even less accountability.

The Irish Penal Reform Trust believes that there is no such thing as a 'good' prison and that ultimately a prison operates as a deformed society which is unarguably and universally damaging, however decent are those administering it. As a campaigning institution therefore, we are grateful to have the opportunity to be able to share with you a basic set of community principles, called restorative justice principles which underlie the work of the Trust and which challenges the notion that prisons are ultimately a solution to crime. Linked to these principles I also want to say a few words about a successful Irish community scheme run by the Gardaí (Irish police) which has been operating since 1963. This programme is about to receive legislative recognition. It is also about to be extended to include a scheme called Family Conferencing which in turn, incorporates restorative justice principles. Before I do all this, I need to say a few words about the changing climate regarding crime in Ireland.

Crime in Ireland

Up to the deaths in 1996 of Garda Gerry McCabe and journalist Veronica Guerin, crime was pretty much a non-event in Ireland - it didn't bother ordinary (middle class) people too much. There was considerable tolerance associated with, in particular, petty and middle class crime. Neither were politicians too concerned - no votes to be had from that direction! However, since the shootings of McCabe and Guerin and due in large measure to hysteria whipped up by the media and latched onto by politicians, we are led to believe that we in Ireland live in a climate of rampant crime. One might be forgiven for thinking that the Irish collective psyche wants nothing but retribution, that is to inflict suffering on those who have made others suffer. Our present Minister for Justice's election promise of zero tolerance and his ongoing promise to build 2,000 new prison places - without any recourse to research - is evidence of this. As against all this, however, we need to acknowledge that Ireland has the lowest crime rate in Europe and most crime, estimated at 80% (or at least the crime that ends up in prison) is drug related and comes from approximately 5 exceptionally poor areas in Dublin.

Paradoxically, however, we also happen to have the highest throughput of prisoners in Europe, the highest recidivism rate, the most expensive prison system - £900 per week per prisoner - and, relevant to this conference, the highest proportion of under 21's in custody. Therefore, since we in the Trust believe that it is almost impossible to train people for freedom in conditions of captivity, consideration of community alternatives to prison is particularly appropriate. We believe that restorative justice rather than this awful type of retributive justice that underlies our prison system is a much better bet.

Restorative Justice

Retributive justice is based on the assumption that if the punishment is sufficiently high it will deter future offending. Clearly this type of punishment doesn't work. One of the reasons may be that prisoners, by definition, are isolated from the consequences of their actions. With retributive justice, both victims and offenders are put in a passive role because the offence is seen primarily as an offence against the state. Restorative Justice, on the other hand, emphasises ways in which crime harms relationships in the context of the community. It is underpinned by three assumptions: firstly, offenders are capable of accepting responsibility for their behaviour; secondly, reparation by offenders to victims is a substantive and healing form of justice for both victim and offender; and thirdly, all communities are entitled to, and are capable of, self-empowerment relative to appropriate preventative crime measures. Possibly one of the most important preventative crime measures are the victim-offender mediation schemes or as they will be known in Ireland, Family Conferencing.

These schemes are a get-together grouping of all those relevant people connected to the juvenile who has already acknowledged his or her crime. These programmes normally aim to realise the following objectives: victims would be offered practical opportunities to regain personal power through having an input into how the harm is practically repaired. Offenders would be obliged to undertake life skills to aid accepting responsibility for their actions as well as repairing the harm done. This programme is oriented to create a sense of ownership by the community. Thus the major goals of restorative justice are: victim empowerment, community involvement and offender responsibility.

In a nutshell then, the current model of retributive justice sees crime as a violation of the state and its laws. It focuses on establishing guilt so that an appropriate measure of pain can be allocated to the offender. The search for guilt is based on conflict between experts such as lawyers and the police. The victim, offender and wider community are largely uninvolved. Restorative justice, on the other hand, sees crime as a violation of people and the relationships between them. Its emphasis is on trying to make right the harm done. Victims and offenders, therefore, are key players in the negotiation of a just settlement.

Howard Zehr, one of the earliest and most influential thinkers and writers in the field, describes the shift from retributive to restorative justice as requiring a 'change of lenses' so that our focus is on the future and solving problems, rather than on the past and allocating blame. This is a useful way of thinking about the leap of imagination required to make the ideas behind restorative justice part of our thinking about responses to crime.

Restorative justice, however, is not just another new programme to be bolted onto the existing system. It is a radically new vision about how to manage crime and treat offenders. One has to be careful of how one particular value system is grafted onto another. Having said that, there are many different schemes being tested in America, Canada, New Zealand, Australia, England and other countries. So far the results are reassuring.

A recent USA study found that family conferencing schemes resulted in very high satisfaction rates for both victims (83%) and offenders (85%). These schemes were also found to reduce fear among victims: before mediation 25% lived in fear of future crime, after mediation 10% thought the offender might re-victimise them. Precisely because of the intense emotional trauma experienced by victims of violence as well as the impact (or lack of it) on the offender, the potential benefits of restorative justice interventions may be enormous. Highly structured and facilitated dialogues between small groups of prisoners of violent crime and victims (not their own victims) have recently been conducted within the prison system in USA, and I believe in a prison in Leeds. It is early days yet but things are looking good.

The Trust believes the Irish culture is particularly suited to restorative justice. There are precedents for alternative methods of dispute resolution. These include the Dáil courts described by Judge Mary Kotsonouris in her book Retreat From Revolution. These courts were established in June 1920, a time when people had abandoned the British system of justice. They were presided over by locally elected justices in virtually every parish and dealt with thousands of disputes, until they were wound up after the civil war. There are also more ancient examples – the Brehon law which preceded the Common Law in this country was based on ideas of compensation, restitution and group culpability.

Finally, the Christian roots of restorative justice would suggest that the idea will have more resonance in Ireland than in more secular (or less homogenous) societies. For all of these reasons I think we can, at least theoretically, be optimistic about the chances of success in Ireland. It is also true to say, I think, that the roots of restorative justice have been silently in place since 1963. I am referring to the Juvenile Liaison Scheme.

Juvenile Liaison Scheme

The Garda Juvenile Diversion Programme was established in 1963 in order to divert juvenile offenders from criminal activity and to provide an alternative to them being processed through the formal criminal justice system. The 1996 Children's Bill proposes that it would operate on a statutory basis. This Diversion Programme operates under the supervision of the Garda National Juvenile Office. It is operated throughout all Garda divisions by specially trained Gardaí who are employed as Juvenile Liaison Officers or, as they are usually called, JLOs. A juvenile offender is dealt with by way of a caution (which may be formal or informal) or by the institution of criminal proceedings. Informal cautions, for usually very minor offences, are administered by the local JLO and is normally done at the offender's home and in the presence of the offender's parents or guardian. A formal caution is administered by the local District Officer and takes places at the Garda station and, again, in the presence of parents or guardians. JLOs meet and co-operate with parents, teachers, probation officers, social workers, welfare officers and personnel involved in child guidance clinics, public health clinics and the courts. They also take an active interest in youth and other clubs operating in the community. JLOs also give talks to schools and other relevant organisations.

In 1996, some 10,539 juvenile offenders were included in the programme bringing the number included since the inception of the programme to a total of 86,195 offenders. Of the total number included in the programme, not surprisingly perhaps, 83% were male and 17% were female. Just to provide you with a sense of scale: since its inception 77,000 juvenile offenders, or 89% of the total, reached their 18th year without re-prosecution. This indicates a definite measure of success. In the same year, JLOs visited 5,663 juvenile offenders who were under intensive supervision and a further 16,579 visits were made to those under regular supervision. In addition, more than 7,000 visits were made to schools and clubs. In 1996 one quarter of juveniles referred to the JLO scheme was between 16-17 years. Slightly worrying, however, is the trend in the type of crime committed since 1995: 21% increase in drink related offences and serious assaults increased by 65%. As noted already, the JLO scheme is to be provided with a statutory basis as part of the 1996 Children's Bill.

1996 Children's Bill

In 1996 the then coalition consisting of Fine Gael (the second largest party in the republic), the Labour Party and the Democratic Left (somewhat euphemistically called parties of the Left) introduced this Bill in an attempt to introduce some formal planning relative to the juvenile justice area. Due to that particular coalition losing the general election in 1997, the Bill originally fell off the order paper but was recently restored in its original format. This means it is now at the committee stage of the Dáil proceedings.

Of particular interest here is the Family Conference Scheme designed to be carried out under the auspices of the Juvenile Liaison Scheme. What is proposed in the Bill is this: the programme is to be carried out and managed by a member of the Gardaí not below the rank of Superintendent who will be known as the Director. The starting point, as in the other JLO scheme, is that the juvenile admits responsibility for his/her offence. S/he is then placed under the care of a juvenile liaison officer who in turn prepares a report in a prescribed form which is submitted to the Director with a recommendation on what action should be taken and a statement on any action that has already been taken. If the Director decides to admit the juvenile to the family conference scheme a category of caution is administered to the juvenile. The JLO gives written notice to the parent or guardian specifying the child's action, the type of caution and the place where this caution is to be administered. A formal caution means that the juvenile is placed under supervision.

The child must accept responsibility for the offence that is alleged to have been committed. He or she must consent to be cautioned and, where appropriate, consent to be supervised. The parents or guardian must agree to attend the conference and, particularly useful, a 'significant other' as well as the victim is invited to attend. The consent of the victim is not essential for admission to the programme. Cautions, either informal or formal, for the most part are to be administered at a Garda station or at the home of the juvenile. The views of the family and the victim are then taken into consideration and the victim is invited to attend the family conference. My understanding is that the conferencing may go ahead should the victim refuse to attend. At the conference attempts are made to understand why the juvenile committed the offence, what effect it had on the victim and what preventative measures need to be taken. A report is subsequently made to the Director which is privileged and may not be used in future court appearances or elsewhere.

There are 150 amendments to the Bill. Relative to family conferencing, here are the kinds of things that are being considered. It is intended that the idea of family conferencing becomes a more integral part of the JLO scheme. Furthermore, after the family conferencing has convened, an action plan will be drawn up and a review is to be set up for approximately 6 months time. Most interestingly, the parents of the offender will be encouraged to take the initiative drawn up in the action plan, whether that be a formal apology, an attempt to do the victim's garden or messages or whatever. If the reparative action looks weak, half-hearted or even absent, then the JLO is provided with the where-with-all to accelerate the reconvening of the next family conferencing. Here the offender will be expected to be accountable for their relative non-action. The threat of going to court will not exist, however. We view this as a good thing as it ultimately must lead to greater creativity and empowerment of both family and community.

So far the picture looks good. But in the view of the Trust there are two aspects to the pending legalisation that are a bit worrying. The first is the place of venue: either in the relevant Garda station or the juvenile's home (except in exceptional circumstances). There may well be an attempt through the amendments to prioritise the home. We would suggest, however, that neither venue can be considered neutral for all too obvious reasons. There are very poor areas where police presence is viewed negatively. Certain homes in this area might see the presence of a conference as a further way of challenging the 'system'. Or, there may even be some families that see the presence of a JLO, and so on, as providing that family with particular quodos! Either way, the situation is a particularly sensitive one.

It would seem that a neutral venue would be a much safer bet. The second potential problem stems from the same source: lack of apparent neutrality relative to the fact that the facilitator or liaison officer is obviously a member of the Gardaí. I appreciate that in the Thames Valley and in Australia the police as facilitators appear to have worked well. Given the Irish culture, however, and stemming from a historical sense of colonialism, perhaps, we need to acknowledge our highly ambiguous attitude to authority. The Trust, therefore, believes that such venues and such facilitating, may well act as a disincentive to successful conferencing. At the very least, we feel, that the legalisation, while not excluding the Gardaí by any means, ought to include other disciplines, such as probation/welfare as well.

Conclusion

The Trust acknowledges that the restorative approach cannot resolve the structural injustices that underlie much crime but at least the measures taken are infinitely more humane and hopeful. I am not saying that there are any simple ways to make our penal system fairer and more effective. What I am saying is that we know the current narrow focus on retribution and prisons has failed, and it is time to think in new ways about tackling crime.

What I have described is eminently achievable. Ireland is said to have the lowest crime rate in Europe. Furthermore, recent statistics indicate that crime is falling further. There is thus hope that the feeling of panic is passing since the deaths of MaCabe and Guerin. The 1996 Children's Bill, we hope, will be a sign of hope. Community involvement, victim and offender satisfaction, the notion of repairing harm done, all of which exists as roots of family conferencing are all deeply embedded within the communitarian aspect of Irish culture - indeed as far back, as noted above, as the Brehon Laws. Paradoxical as we intend to be this exists in tandem with the deeply retributive notion recently made explicit by our present government: zero tolerance . We, in the Trust, believe that at least a partial return to the positive values of community is potentially explicit in this 1996 Children's Bill. If it is passed then we may no longer be able to boast of the highest prison input and the highest proportion of under 21s in custody in Europe. If all this comes about then, as citizens, we might also be relieved that we will no longer have one of the most expensive - and ineffective - prison systems in Europe.

EXPLORING DIVERSITY: UNDERSTANDING AND RESPONDING TO OFFENDING AMONG YOUNG WOMEN AND GIRLS

Professor Gill McIvor, Director of Social Research Centre, University of Stirling, Scotland

---

Introduction

The issue of gender and crime - or, more specifically, female offending - has traditionally received scant attention by academics and by policy-makers. Arguably this is because women constitute a relatively small proportion of offenders who appear before the courts. The consequence is that our current understanding of offending among children and young people has been derived largely from studies of young men and boys. More significantly, perhaps, the systems and approaches which have been developed to respond to offending among young people have been based upon a highly gendered conceptualisation of crime and delinquency which, in turn, tends to limit their appropriateness for young women and girls.

In this short paper I will do three things.

◆ First, I will consider what we know empirically about gender differences in offending and the implications for our understanding of offending by young people.

◆ Next, I will examine gender differences in the processing of male and female offenders by the criminal justice system, drawing in part upon data derived from Scottish research and with an emphasis upon the differential adoption of welfare and justice approaches as a framework for understanding the differences which emerge.

◆ Finally, I will consider the implications of recent policy initiatives in Scotland which have served to focus attention upon the circumstances and experiences of young women in the criminal justice system.

Gender and offending

Turning first to gender and offending, a pattern of gender differences emerges which is broadly consistent across western jurisdictions:

1. Boys are more likely to offend than girls, though this difference - or what has been referred to as the gender ratio - is less marked in self-report studies than in analyses based upon official data.

2. Boys tend to commit offences more frequently than girls.

3.   The difference in rates of offending between boys and girls is less marked for less serious offences and more marked for serious property offences and violent crime. i.e. boys tend to commit more serious offences than girls.

Against this backdrop of difference, however, there are some interesting similarities in the pattern of offending between young men and women which theories attempting to embrace gender in explanations of criminality must address:

1.   Although boys more often commit trivial offences and more serious offences than girls, both boys and girls commit trivial offences most often and serious offences rarely.

2.   A similar pattern of age-related offending occurs among young men and women. An analysis of criminal convictions by age and gender, for example, led Stuart Asquith and Elaine Samuel (1994) to conclude that "for females, as well as for males, crime is very much a youth related phenomenon in Scotland". They then continue thus:

> the great gender difference in actual numbers of convictions is possibly responsible for overlooking the age-related pattern of offending behaviour amongst females. To overlook or ignore this pattern, however, helps sustain the myth of female criminality as individualistic, pathological and essentially non-social.

The significance of gender is also relevant when considering the risk factors for offending behaviour. Here, the majority of studies have tended to focus upon the risk factors for male offending, perhaps with the implicit assumption that similar factors which are relevant to boys will apply in respect of girls. There is, indeed, some evidence that the risk factors for boys and girls may overlap. For example, Simourd and Andrews (1994), in a meta-analysis of studies exploring risk factors and delinquency, found that the same risk factors, in the same order of significance, were important for female and male delinquency, with none of these risk factors appearing to be more important for one gender for another:

♦   antisocial attitudes and peers;
♦   temperament or misconduct problems;
♦   emotional difficulties;
♦   educational difficulties;
♦   poor parent-child relations.

However, Simourd and Andrews acknowledge that existing studies may not have considered a range of variables that may potentially differentiate between boys and girls with respect to risk. For example, child sexual abuse may be a more significant risk factor for girls than for boys: we know, for instance, that imprisoned women more often disclose a history of sexual abuse than do imprisoned men. It has also been suggested that for girls, child sexual abuse may contribute to the commission of status offences such as running away which may in turn provide a pathway to offending behaviours such as drug abuse and prostitution.

45

Even if the risk factors for delinquency among boys and girls are broadly similar, the question arises as to why girls offend less often than boys. Two possible explanations have been put forward:

1.   boys are more exposed to certain risk factors than girls by virtue of the closer supervision afforded the latter

2.   boys and girls respond differently to particular risk factors.

There is certainly some support for both of these hypotheses. For instance, there is evidence that girls offend in fewer settings than boys and that when they offend in settings that are not usual for them they tend to do so at a relatively high rate.

Second, there is some evidence that girls are more likely to respond to emotional problems through a process of internalisation which is manifest in anxiety, depression and self-injurious behaviour. Boys, on the other hand, are more likely to respond by what might collectively be defined as overt acting-out behaviours, including various manifestations of delinquency.

Turning, to the issue of gender and criminological theory, two broad approaches have typically been adopted to explain female offending:

1.   the first has been to subsume women under general theories of crime which have been developed to account for offending among males.

2.   the second has been to develop alternative explanations which often stem from some of the obvious differences between men and women in society.

The difficulty with both approaches, however, is that neither can adequately accommodate both similarity and difference between male and female offending. Traditional criminological theories can better address the similarities in offending between men and women but are hard pushed to account adequately for the differences.

There has, in addition, been little empirical support for a range of theoretical perspectives which attempt to explain female offending with reference to concepts such as sex role maladjustment, emancipation, masculinity and hormonal or other biological factors.

Other theories based upon gender differences, such as feminist theories, are better able to account for phenomena such as the gender ratio in offending but are less adequately equipped to explain some of the striking similarities in offending patterns between women and men, such as the relationship between criminal convictions and age.

Any adequate theory of criminality must, I would suggest, be able to accommodate both similarity and difference with respect to gender and offending. It should reflect the distinctiveness of female and male experiences - and, where relevant, their commonalities - and should also be capable of offering answers to the following questions:

- why, if the main risk factors for boys and girls are similar, are boys more likely than girls to offend, to do so more frequently and to commit more serious offences?

- why, despite the large gender ratio, is offending among boys and girls a strongly age-related phenomenon?

It is also important to recognise that different explanatory frameworks are likely to be required to account for offending at different ages. Offending amongst boys and girls, especially offending of a relatively minor nature, is I would argue, linked to a range of other risk-taking behaviours which in turn are associated with the search for identity in the transition from adolescence to adulthood. Offending among young adults, on the other hand, is often more utilitarian in nature or precipitated by other problems and stresses. In Scotland, for instance clear gender differences are found in the patterns of adult offending, with women more likely than men to be convicted of failure to pay for a TV licence, prostitution, shoplifting and fraud while men are more likely than women to be convicted of violent crimes, indecency and dishonesty offences such as housebreaking and car theft (Scottish Office, 1998).

Criminal justice responses to offending

Whilst self-report studies tend to support the view that most girls **do** offend, the majority of young people who are processed through the criminal justice system are male. This may partly be accounted for by the fact that young women who offend do so less frequently than their male counterparts, putting them less often at risk of detection and arrest **or** it may reflect the fact that boys tend to commit more serious offences than girls. However, there is also evidence of differential responses by criminal justice agencies to different types of offending by boys and girls, with US data, for instance suggesting that girls are processed more harshly than boys for status offences, while they are treated less harshly than boys for criminal offences.

There has also been a tendency for offending among girls to be sexualised, with protective measures invoked within a welfare framework which emphasises needs as opposed to deeds. The recent Scottish Office report on women offenders, for example, noted that many girls referred to the children's hearing system on offence grounds were also referred for truancy, being beyond parental control and being in 'moral danger'. Offending girls were also more likely than offending boys to come to the attention of the children's hearing system for being the victim of an offence such as sexual abuse, as well as being beyond parental control or in 'moral danger'. The report concludes that 'being a victim of abuse or neglect does not necessarily lead to offending but that girls who offend are more likely than boys to be victims as well' (Scottish Office, 1998, p. 12).

The existence of a more welfare based criminal justice response to offending by young women is reflected in patterns of sentencing in the adult court. Lizanne Dowds and Carol Hedderman (1997), for example, found that courts in England and Wales were reluctant to impose fines upon female offenders. In some cases this appeared to result in a more lenient response, in comparison with male offenders, by way of a discharge: in other cases it appeared that women may have been escalated up the sentencing tariff through the imposition of a community sentence in lieu of a fine.

Women have been consistently under-represented on community service schemes. Thus in 1994 women accounted for 14 per cent of persons sentenced by the courts in Scotland but only 7 per cent of those given a community service order (Scottish Office, 1995a). A similar picture is found in England and Wales (Hine 1993). Moreover gender differences in the relative use of community service are greatest among younger offenders. For example in Scotland in 1993, 16-17 year old males were more than three times as likely to receive community service than were young women of the same age while young men aged between 18 and 24 years were twice as likely as young women in the same age group to receive this particular sentencing option (Scottish Office, 1995b).

It is on the basis of findings such as these that Anne Worrall (1995) has suggested that community service is permeated by the ideology that it is a 'young man's punishment' and, as such, is a highly gendered disposal. Asquith and Samuel (1994) have also suggested that community service does not fit with the 'conventional view of female offenders which finds them needy, not fully responsible for their actions, and requiring, above all else, special protection and support' arguing that 'as long as the welfare model predominates, then female offenders will be in prison for offences which do not justify incarceration' (p.77). In support of their argument, Asquith and Samuel report that in 1988 16-17 year-old females against whom a charge was proved in Scottish courts were five times more likely to receive a custodial sentence than a community service order. Males of the same age, on the other hand, were only twice as likely to be detained in custody than ordered to perform community service.

Although there is some evidence that when age, current offence and criminal history are controlled for, women are as likely to receive community service as men (Mair and Brockington, 1988) and that women who are referred for community service assessments are as likely to receive a community service order as men (Scottish Office, 1995b) there are, nonetheless, clear differences in the characteristics of men and women referred for and sentenced to community service. In a recent study of community service referrals to three Scottish courts (McIvor, forthcoming), I found clear gender differences with respect to a number of variables which are generally recognised as being associated with the risk of a custodial sentence being imposed. Men, for instance, were more likely to have been remanded in custody prior to conviction while women were more likely to have been ordained; women on the other hand were more likely to be first offenders were less likely previously to have served a custodial sentence. In addition to having less extensive offending histories, women were also found to be more often facing sentence less serious offences. Men were almost twice as likely as women to have been thought by the social worker preparing the SER to be at risk of attracting a sentence of detention or imprisonment and, while social workers more often found it difficult to form a clear judgement concerning custody risk in the case of women offenders, women were more often than men thought not to be at risk.

The available evidence thus points clearly to differences in the characteristics of men and women considered for and sentenced to community service and to differential access to community service for male and female offenders. These differences may result from decisions reached at various points in the sentencing process and may reflect a variety of factors, including the conceptualisation of community service as a young man's punishment and an emphasis upon the domestic responsibilities of women offenders which precludes them from being considered suitable for a community service order.

Consistent with a more general observation that a welfare approach tends to underpin responses to offending among women and girls, we find that probation orders have traditionally been imposed more often upon women offenders than upon men, though since 1991 the proportions of male and female offenders given probation orders in Scotland have been equal: in 1995 probation orders were made in respect of 4 per cent and men and women who were sentenced in Scottish courts (Scottish Office, 1997). In 1991 the Scottish Office introduced National Objectives and Standards for social work services to the criminal justice system (Social Work Services Group, 1991). With respect to probation supervision, they encouraged a shift from a more traditional welfare approach focused primarily upon offenders' needs to what has been variously referred to as a justice (McIvor and Barry, 1998) or responsibility model (Paterson and Tombs, 1998) in which the task of addressing offending behaviour takes precedence. This shift in emphasis may, it is suggested, offer at least a partial explanation for the erosion of the gender difference in the use of the probation order in Scotland.

Nonetheless a study of probation supervision in Scotland following the introduction of full central government funding and national objectives and standards revealed marked differences in the focus and content of probation supervision with male and female offenders (McIvor, 1997). With the former, the emphasis was more often upon offending behaviour and other problem behaviours - such as drug or alcohol abuse - that might actively contribute to a risk of continued offending. With women, the offending which had resulted in the imposition of the probation order was not ignored, but the approach of social workers to the supervision of women was more likely than in their work with men to focus on resolving practical or material problems and providing probationers with emotional and social support. Moreover a comparison of the characteristics of men and women made subject to probation suggested that women were less likely than men to have been diverted from a custodial sentence by a probation order: welfare concerns had, it seems, continued to influence the choice of probation as a disposal for female offenders.

Whilst there is a danger that the welfare model might, unless workers are alert to its discriminatory potential, serve to sustain and promulgate unhelpful stereotyped views of women offenders, it is also instructive to consider the extent to which the practice adopted by social workers in this study was viewed by the women themselves as addressing their needs. The nine women interviewed did not consider themselves to be 'criminals' and valued practical help aimed at enabling them to take greater control over their lives. Empowerment was a key theme, with most women describing the process by which they had been enabled through probation to become more assertive in their personal relationships, to pay more attention to meeting their own needs and to begin making decisions for themselves. Social workers - in all but one instance women themselves - did not encourage the women to become dependent on them, but helped them gain the confidence and self-esteem to start re-building their lives. Women did not, in general, want their social workers to do things and make decisions for them: they wanted options and the confidence to begin taking responsibility for themselves.

The picture painted through the accounts of these female probationers appears to call into question the appropriateness for women of probation practice based on a justice model, with its attendant emphasis upon offending behaviour and strict adherence to standards. As Anne Worrall (1995) and others (e.g. Jones et al., 1991) have indicated, women probationers do not readily relate to a contractual model of supervision including, for instance, compulsory attendance at groupwork sessions (Beaumont and Mistry, 1996) even if, for some of the women in the Scottish study, the framework of regular appointments apparently served to enhance their motivation to effect and sustain positive change.

The problem with the adoption of a dual approach to probation supervision - in which welfare concerns predominate in respect of women offenders and a justice model is applied in respect of men - is linked to the concept of proportionality and to the risk that women may be subject to tariff escalation if they fail to successfully complete their probation orders or if they re-offend. What, arguably, is required, is the availability of a graduated response by the courts which recognises and embraces the nature and circumstances of women's offending. The current tariff system represents such a graduated response - albeit with its imperfections - to offending by men but its relevance to women's offending is increasingly being questioned. The reluctance of the courts to fine women offenders or to make use of community service for women offenders who are at risk of custody effectively removes important steps from the penalogical ladder.

There is a need for more imaginative approaches to women offenders through, for instance, the increased use - where appropriate - of diversion from prosecution, supervised attendance orders, voluntary supervision and supervision in the context of a deferred sentence. In other words, responses which are inclusionary in intent and which recognise both the minor and transitory nature of much offending by women and the economic, social and personal circumstances in which that offending occurs.

A future agenda for research and policy

The issue of gender has been ignored to a significant extent in studies of offending among young people, most of which - such as longitudinal studies in England and in North America - have focused upon populations of young males. As such, the relevance of insights which have been derived from these studies to an understanding of female offending has yet to be explored. However, if female offending is to be better understood and more appropriately responded to, a number of issues need to be addressed:

For example, there is now some evidence that even where boys and girls commit similar types of offences, the contexts in which they offend may be different. Therefore, information about the context of offending - where, who with, how - is necessary to address the question of whether boys and girls do indeed offend in similar ways or whether there are important gender differences in this respect.

It will also be necessary to take cognisance of the potentially complex interplay of issues such as gender, ethnicity and social context both in influencing offending **and** in influencing responses to it. How do these variables interact and what is their relative significance in terms of how young people behave and how formal agencies respond to these behaviours?

In Scotland there is increasing academic interest in the issue of female offending. The significance of gender is being explored, for instance, in the longitudinal study of young people and crime being conducted by colleagues in the Centre for Law and Society at the University of Edinburgh, while colleagues at Glasgow University have recently received funding from the ESRC for a study of violence among young women and girls. I am currently involved with colleagues in the Social Work Research Centre at the University of Stirling in a major study of resistance to, desistance from and persistence in offending behaviour among young people of different ages in two Scottish towns in which a primary focus is upon gender. Here we are exploring similarities and differences in offending among young men and young women and are examining the significance of concepts such as identity and masculinity in respect of young people and crime.

The increasing academic interest in female offending and female offenders has been mirrored by increased policy interest in this issue, triggered by the tragic suicides at Cornton Vale women's prison. Last month the Scottish Office published a review of community disposals and the use of custody for women offenders in Scotland. It has elsewhere been suggested that 'imprisoned women are usually marginalised women sharing characteristics that are devalued by society' (Bloom et al., 1995, p.132). The marginal status of women prisoners has been highlighted in studies in the United States (Owen and Bloom, 1995), Canada (Shaw, 1994) and Australia (Edwards, 1995) and in recent studies of women prisoners in England and Wales (Morris et al., 1995; Caddle and Crisp, 1997) and in Scotland (Loucks, 1998). In comparison with men, women prisoners are more likely to have a history of physical or sexual abuse and are more likely to self harm (Dembo et al., 1993; Leibling, 1994). Moreover, imprisonment often serves to further weaken or destroy women's existing ties to the community (Wilkinson, 1988; Eaton, 1993). As the Scottish Office report concludes, 'the backgrounds of women in prison are characterised by experiences of abuse, drug misuse, poor educational attainment, poverty, psychological distress and self harm' (Scottish Office, 1998, p.13).

The Scottish Office report is, therefore, to be commended for its recommendations aimed at reducing the use of custody for women offenders, whether at the remand stage, as a response to fine default or upon first sentence. With respect to young offenders, the report recommends further that by the year 2000 no young women under 18 years of age should be held in prison establishments, with use being made instead of secure accommodation for this age group.

Other recommendations in the Scottish Office report include the development of bail provision for women who have been accused of an offence; the development of a unitary fine system; the increased use of supervised attendance orders for women who default on payment of their fines; the development of an inter-agency project aimed at developing services for women offenders in Glasgow; a review of social work provision for women offenders across Scotland; the collation and publishing of statistics on women offenders from the year 2000 onwards; and a revision of the Scottish prison service's estates strategy for women to encourage the doubling up of vulnerable prisoners and the and the creation of facilities for women prisoners beyond Cornton Vale.

A delicate balance must be struck when considering the issue of female offending. On the one hand, one must be cautious not to demonise women offenders by exaggerating the nature and scale of female offending. On the other hand, there is a need for offending among women and girls to be better understood in order that more appropriate and effective responses can be developed and potential sources of discriminatory practice addressed. It is my hope that developments which follow on from the publication of the Scottish Office report will achieve the right balance and will result in the provision of services for young women who offend which are both effective and appropriate to their needs.

References

Asquith, S. and Samuel, E. (1994) *Review of Criminal Justice and Related Services for Young Adult Offenders*, Edinburgh: HMSO.

Beaumont, B. and Mistry, T. (1996) Doing a good job under duress, *Probation Journal, 43, 4*, 200-204.

Bloom, B., Immarigeon, R. and Owen, B. (1995) Editorial introduction, *The Prison Journal, 75, 2*, 131-4.

Caddle, D. and Crisp, D. (1997) *Imprisoned Women and Mothers*, HORS 162, London: The Home Office.

Dembo, R., Williams, L. and Schmeidler, J. (1993) Gender differences in mental health service needs among youth entering a juvenile detention center, Journal of *Prison and Jail Health, 12, 2*, 73-101.

Dowds, L. and Hedderman, C. (1997) The sentencing of men and women, in C. Hedderman and L. Gelsthorpe (Eds) *Understanding the Sentencing of Women*, Home Office Research Study 170, London: Home Office.

Eaton, M. (1993) *Women After Prison*, Buckingham: Open University Press.

Edwards, A. (1995) *Women in Prison*, Sydney: New South Wales Bureau of Crime Statistics and Research.

Hine, J. (1993) Access for women: Flexible and friendly? in D. Whitfield and D. Scott (Eds.) *Paying Back: Twenty Years of Community Service*, Winchester: Waterside Press.

Jones, M., Mordecai, M., Rutter, F. and Thomas, L. (1991) The Miskin Model of groupwork with women offenders, *Groupwork, 4,* 215-230.

Leibling, A. (1994) Suicide among women prisoners, *The Howard Journal, 33, 1,* 1-9.
Mair, G. and Brockington, N. (1988) Female offenders and the probation service, *The Howard Journal, 27, 2,* 117-126.

McIvor, G. (1997) *Gender differences in probation practice in Scotland*, paper presented at the British Criminology Conference, The Queen's University Belfast.

McIvor, G. (forthcoming) Jobs for the boys?: Gender differences in referral for community service, *The Howard Journal.*

McIvor, G. and Barry, M. (1998) *Social Work and Criminal Justice Volume 6: Probation,* Edinburgh: The Stationery Office.

Morris, A., Wilkinson, C., Tisi, A., Woodrow, J. and Rockley, A. (1995) *Managing the Needs of Female Prisoners,* London: The Home Office.

Owen, B. and Bloom, B. (1995) Profiling women prisoners: Findings from national surveys and a California sample, *The Prison Journal, 75, 2,* 165-85.

Paterson, F. and Tombs, J. (1998) *Social Work and Criminal Justice Volume 1: The Impact of Policy,* Edinburgh: The Stationery Office.

Scottish Office (1995a) *Statistical Bulletin: Criminal Proceedings in Scottish Courts 1994,* Edinburgh: The Scottish Office.

Scottish Office (1995b) *Statistical Bulletin: Community Service by Offenders in 1992 and 1993,* Edinburgh: The Scottish Office.

Scottish Office (1997) *Statistical Bulletin: Criminal Proceedings in Scottish Courts 1995,* Edinburgh: The Scottish Office.

Scottish Office (1998) *Women Offenders - A Safer Way: A Review of Community Disposals and the Use of Custody for Women Offenders in Scotland,* Edinburgh: The Stationery Office.

Shaw, M. (1994) Women in prison: A literature review, *Forum on Corrections, 6, 1,* Canadian Department of Corrections.

Simourd, L. and Andrews, D.A. (1994) Correlates of delinquency: A look at gender differences, *Forum on Corrections, 6,* 1.

Social Work Services Group (1991) *National Objectives and Standards for Social Work Services in the Criminal Justice System,* Edinburgh: The Scottish Office.

Wilkinson, C. (1988) The post-release experience of female prisoners, in A. Morris and C. Wilkinson (Eds.) *Women and the Penal System,* Cambridge: University of Cambridge Institute of Criminology.

Worrall, A. (1995) Gender, criminal justice and probation, in G. McIvor (Ed.) *Working with Offenders: Research Highlights in Social Work 26,* London: Jessica Kingsley.

DEALING WITH DIVERSITY IN THE COURT

Lynne Ravenscroft, Magistrates Association, England

Introduction

In 1976 when I became a magistrate, the proportion of men to women was about 60:40. Now it is about 53:47. Since women have only been able to be on the Bench for 78 years, to have achieved near parity in that time is remarkable given that the chaps had been lording it on their own for nearly 600 years before then, and given that positive discrimination must have taken place to achieve this; we should note that neither the courts nor the magistracy is in a state of collapse. I am not suggesting that any earth-shattering improvements have taken place since the arrival of women magistrates, though I am quite sure they must have done, but there is very little specific research based on the gender composition of the Bench, though I am sad to say that what little there has been, by Anne Worral (1983) in *Sisters in Law*, tended to suggest that:

"women magistrates are socially constructed within a number of discourses, in such a way that they can claim to be both similar to (for the purpose of special and authoritative understanding) and different from (for the purpose of sentencing) women defendants."

Criminologists suggest this is the Madonna/Whore response to women defendants. That is, if she appears as a stereotypical polite, respectful, gentle woman she will be treated more leniently than a man, but if she appears as a tough, hard more masculine character she will be treated more harshly than a man would be.

Glass ceilings would not appear to limit the aspirations of women magistrates: in my own county of six Benches, half the chairs are women. The last three chairs of the Magistrates' Association have been women. Whilst there is no statutory requirement for a mix of sexes in the ordinary petty sessions, there must be very good reasons for there not being so in the Youth Court or the Family Proceedings Court.

I am not referring to the other Criminal Justice agencies - we must deal with what comes before us in the court. I am going to spend some time dealing with just who magistrates are because I believe that may help to explain what prejudices they may or may not have, and all of us here have some; and whether they impinge on their work in the courts; and then I am going to talk about a new training programme that is designed to help them - us - in guarding against any form of discrimination in the courts.

Who's Who in the Youth Courts and How Diverse are We?

You all know the accusation - we are white, middle aged, middle class and male. We are appointed as law-abiding citizens with the time to give and an interest in the criminal justice system and we should reflect the community we serve. Most of us do a morning a week in Court and are not paid, though those who are employed claim loss of earnings. These factors alone may well limit those who choose to apply but many people may not be aware that they can apply, and most certainly do not have to wait to be asked, as was true not so long ago. Except in London we are all magistrates who sit in the Adult Courts as well as in the Youth Courts, about one third of the total of magistrates do that. We are selected to sit in the Youth Courts because of our special interest in or knowledge of young people. Until the 1991 Criminal Justice Act, we had to retire from the Youth Panel when 65, now it is the same as the adult court, 70.

The Lord Chancellor's Department in December 1997 produced a clear document entitled 'Disabled Court Users' Good Practice Guide' in which it states the standards that Magistrates Courts Committees must meet for the provision of facilities for disabled court users in order for them to discharge their responsibilities for the efficient and effective administration of the magistrates' courts in their area. The advice is not simply about ramps, Hearing loops or Braille books but includes comments about the appropriate behaviour towards someone who is a wheelchair user, is blind, has a learning disability, and so forth, so that no-one is disadvantaged by the courtroom setting, and that includes magistrates. The present Lord Chancellor has approved the appointment of six blind magistrates.

In a speech to the Magistrates' Association's Annual General Meeting last October, Lord Irvine said that he proposed to appoint more Labour voters to the Bench. This was not an attempt to bring politics into the judiciary but rather to ensure that the lay Bench is a true reflection of the communities it serves. Every magistrate is required from time to time to inform the Lord Chancellor's Department of their political inclinations, if they have them, in order to ensure that there is a balance of political views.

Any discourse on the subject of diversity should include the question of sexual orientation. I am not aware of any research into the treatment of gays and lesbians by the courts, nor into their representation on the Bench. Anecdotally I can say that I have some serious concerns about such matters: I do not think homophobia is a problem on our more cosmopolitan Benches but I cannot say the same for others. Incidentally, the word homophobia is not even in my 1959 Oxford English Dictionary. Having just read the Wolfenden Report, I guess we have to remind ourselves that consenting homosexual acts in private were illegal until the 1967 Sexual Offences Act, after nearly 12 years of continuous debate, and which set the age of consent at 21. It is worth noting that Lord Arran, who had moved the original bill in the House of Lords, suggested that: "Homosexuals must remember, while there may be nothing bad in being a homosexual, there is certainly nothing good." Against that background, and bearing in mind that the majority of magistrates are aged 50 plus, it may go some way to explain my fears about homophobia on the Bench.

One of the most disturbing features of the Criminal Justice system is the disproportionate number of people from ethnic minority groups entering it, and in particular being incarcerated in our prisons. Successive Lord Chancellors have grappled with this problem and through the Judicial Studies Board have sought to provide specific training to eliminate any form of discrimination by the judiciary and to increase appointments to both the lay and professional Benches from ethnic communities. Given that 5.8 per cent of the population is from ethnic communities, both the magistrates courts staff and legal advisers are nearly in proportion to that, but the magistracy as a whole is only about 2 per cent. However, new appointments in 1996 included some 6.5 per cent from the ethnic communities. Less than 1 per cent from ethnic communities are represented at the circuit judge level and there are none at the higher levels. Solicitors and barristers are represented at the 6 per cent and 8 per cent levels respectively.

Every magistrate and judge before they can sit in Court must take the judicial oath - *to do right to all manner of people after the laws and usage of this realm without fear or favour, affection or ill will.*

Everyone charged with the duty of seeing that magistrates are fully aware of the meaning of equal treatment issues has to challenge magistrates about their understanding of that oath that they have sworn. No wonder it is one of the hardest tasks of all, and this has been recognised by the Judicial Studies Board which commissioned the NACRO Race and Criminal Justice Unit to produce a major training pack entitled "Equal Treatment Training for Lay Magistrates". This has just been published and is to be used as an integral part of all training to be given to magistrates. Under the new style of general training for the magistracy, magistrates, through rigorous appraisal, will have to demonstrate that they have understood and recognised the effects of discrimination on the basis of race, creed, colour, religion, ethnicity, gender, class, disability, or sexual orientation which can lead to unequal treatment of people in the magistrates' courts."

Many will argue whether there is a gender bias in the Criminal Justice System. What there can be no doubt about is the perception by a significant number of the general public who believes that the criminal justice system does not treat everyone equally. The British Social Attitudes surveys found that in both 1990 and 1994 around 41 per cent of whites believed that a black defendant was more likely than a white defendant to be found guilty in court; the proportion of blacks believing the same rose from 66 per cent to 72 per cent. As the Lord Chief Justice recently wrote:

"Race Issues go to the heart of our criminal justice system, which demands that all are treated as equals before the law. It is a matter of grave concern if members of the ethnic minorities feel they are discriminated against by the criminal justice system: more so if their fears were to be borne out in reality".

According to the 1995 Prison Statistics, when foreign nationals and children under 16 are excluded, the incarceration rate for whites in England and Wales was 135 per 100,000 population; yet the rate for those of Afro-Caribbean origin was 1,049 per 100,000. As Graham and Bowling found in 1995, there is no evidence of a link between inherent criminality and skin colour. Roger Hood's *Race and Sentencing*, a study of 3,317 men and women sentenced in five Crown Court Centres in 1989, found the greatest disparity existed within the band of cases described as being of medium seriousness; there were no differences in the use of custody for black and white defendants aged under 21.

In acknowledging the existence of ethnic minority issues, one is not asking for special privileges for any group. This was enshrined in law as long ago as 1852 in the case of R v Barronett, a Frenchman who had killed a man in a duel and demanded bail saying it was not an offence in France. Rather more recently, in 1974, the position was confirmed in the case of Bradford Corporation v Patel, when a Muslim was found guilty of refusing to send his daughter to a co-educational school but the sentence was mitigated.

The principles are simple and of long standing. Like persons are to be treated in a like manner; unlike persons are to be treated in a manner that takes due account of the differences between them. The law and the criminal justice system afford different treatment to people to reduce discrimination and to promote equality. Sikhs are allowed to carry a knife as part of their uniform. This is not an unwarranted privilege but guarantees equal opportunity whatever the religion. Identical treatment would reinforce inequality. Judges do take account of a number of ethnic values. In the case of Bibi in 1980, the defendant was a Kenyan Asian widow and was convicted of importing cannabis by opening a parcel sent from Kenya. She was sentenced to 3 years imprisonment, reduced on appeal to 6 months, as she was totally dependent on her brother-in-law, real Muslim dependence and she had very little contact with the outside world.

On a broader front, the Courts have a duty to take into account the differing means of defendants appearing before them. Thus, all motorists must obey the Road Traffic Acts but will receive different financial penalties according to their incomes.

The Judicial Studies Board's Equal Treatment Training Pack is a thoroughly comprehensive manual designed to equip all magistrates to fulfil their obligations under the judicial oath. There are exercises designed to cover each of the major stages of decision-making in the Magistrates Courts where discretion is exercised. As Rosemary Thompson, a former colleague of mine on the Magistrates' Association Council wrote in the Magistrate in 1992,

"There is no doubt that the potential for racial discrimination does exist in magistrates' courts as elsewhere and chairmen should be aware of areas where such potential might be found. Examples include bail decisions, requests for pre-sentence reports, adoption of non-custodial recommendations and the use of custodial sentences."

This new pack embraces all forms of discrimination, as is consistent with our international obligations under the Universal Declaration of Human Rights; the International Convention on the Elimination of all forms of Racial Discrimination; the European Convention for the Protection of Human Rights and Fundamental Freedoms; and our own newly to be created Human Rights Act. The purpose of this training for all lay magistrates is to ensure a greater equality of treatment for all who appear in the magistrates' courts, irrespective of their race, gender, ethnic background, colour, creed, religion, social group, disability, or sexual orientation.

I will leave you with this question. What do you suppose the magistrates sitting with a blind colleague will say to them about the defendant in the dock once they have had this training, if not before?

DEALING WITH DIVERSITY - THE WELSH PERSPECTIVE

Sue Thomas, Cynnydd, Wales

Introduction

The first thing I had to ask myself when preparing for this presentation was what diversity means when working in Wales. When we traditionally think about issues of equality for those travelling through the criminal justice system, our focus tends to be on race, sex, gender, ethnicity, etc. I wanted to think whether these would be the foremost issues for us working within the youth justice system in Wales, and have come to the conclusion that whilst it is important and essential that they permeate everything we do in promoting, developing and implementing good practice, there are other issues equally valid that have a particular flavour for us.

These are notably considering the linguistic nature of the country, the make up of different communities - the South Wales valleys, urban and rural areas and how national and local government issues, which often reflect metropolitan models and thinking, affect us in Wales.

With this in mind I would like to expand further and talk specifically about:

- Rurality
- The Welsh Language
- The Impact of Local Government Re-organisation

I am probably going to raise a range of issues for which I do not necessarily provide answers. But I guess that these should all form part of the general debate.

Rurality

The first and most obvious point is that Wales is a largely rural country - remote farms, single dwellings, isolated villages, collapsed industrial areas and coastal areas all comprise its rurality. Powys is the largest county in Wales - Welshpool to Ystradgynlais is a distance of 102 miles and takes 2¼ hours by car.

Rurality presents particular problems, for example:

- individuals with criminal records tend to be highly visible and become stigmatised as trivial offences are often headline news. Local communities know everything:

  " there is real old gossip in the village ready to grass you up, like the time some old bag saw me driving down the road in a friends car and reported me to the police, and the time a friend and I broke into the cricket pavilion for something to do and in the morning the whole village knew who did it" (a rueful young man)

- young people who are highly visible will rapidly come to the attention of the police, in some instances for more minor offences, which can be considered a greater problem in a small community, than they would in a similar situation in an urban context.

- there are limited opportunities for employment and housing and rural areas lack the broad range of services and would expect to find in any urban area.

- the isolation of individuals will also mean that they are unlikely to know what services exist, or how to access them.

- public transport tends to be patchy and expensive to use, again limiting choice.

These factors present significant difficulties in providing a full range of youth justice services. In the first instance discrimination on the ground of where someone lives is wholly improper. A major problem for youth justice services is limited resources and specifically the lack of economies of scale. It is expensive to provide services in remote rural areas for widely dispersed users; even where services are available there is likely to be little or no choice. The national youth agency's point on rural young people sums this up:

> "..... their numbers are not sufficient for them to create the demand that their urban counterparts can exert on... providers by sheer weight of vocal numbers ... market forces ensure that resources are directed at the majority of consumers" (National Youth Agency, 1994)

The main focus for youth justice teams is how to effectively delivery the full range of youth justice services to wide ranging rural communities. Travelling over long distances means that travelling time is inevitably part of the working day. Less young people can be seen or visited. As a result services can not be delivered to as many young people and offending behaviour may not be dealt with as soon as it could. This also manifests itself in maintaining contact and follow up work.

It is virtually impossible to deal with special needs due to low numbers, long distances and lack of transport. Two or three people will not justify the cost of setting up and running a project. As a result you will not find many motor projects, or treatment programmes for young people who sexually abuse in rural areas. Those living in towns and cities are likely to be able to access a much wider range of provision to meet their own particular needs. If this is true in terms of meeting the needs of young men who in the main comprise young offenders, then young women's needs, despite many good intentions, are likely to receive much less attention.

Geographical distances generally mean that young people will have to be routinely seen in their own environments rather than having the opportunity to link into groups, networks or support activities taking place at a location some distance away. Services tend to be more accessible and widespread near urban locations. The further you move away the less there is on offer in terms of accommodation options, employment, educational activities, etc.

Where services do exist there are different implications. For example, there is an attendance centre in Llandudno, which in theory is a sentencing option for young people who live in

North West Wales. However it is totally inaccessible for those living in East Gwynnedd, when the time it would take to get young people there and back is taken into account.

So although an appropriate provision exists it is not an option that is open to certain young people purely because of where they live. The impact of this is that an important stage in the sentencing process is unavailable, which could mean the imposition of a more severe penalty, when a less severe one would have been more appropriate. As a result young people are moved up the sentencing tariff - hence the term justice by geography

Rurality means less likelihood of access to diversion, whether it is in the form of youth liaison panels and cautioning or purely in the provision of community based activities such as cinemas, youth clubs etc which all provide somewhere to go and something to do

Rural courts often sit less frequently than their urban counterparts. They may, for example, sit on a fortnightly or monthly basis. This will inevitably mean that cases take longer to come to court, reducing the immediacy of justice. This does not exactly fit with the current model contained in the Crime and Disorder Bill of fast tracking and speedier justice. Delays may allow time for further offending in the interim.

The rationalisation of the justice system has also meant the closure of courts in rural areas. For example East Gwent has just three courts sitting. Many of the South Wales valleys have courts sitting in central locations rather than on a localised basis.

The transport infrastructure frequently presents difficulties in getting to court for the 10.00am start. For example a young person attending court in Chepstow actually needs to start travelling the day before, as it involves a tortuous route of changing buses which can only be achieved by a detour into Newport (where the local bus station is). We are not talking the wilds of Mid or of North Wales here, but the relative civility of the South Wales/ English Border.

Limited local resources are also likely to impact on young people on remand. For example, it is hard to recruit and maintain foster carers if they are likely to be used infrequently. Remand fostering may not be an option that is used and may result in young people being placed in residential placements when a community option would have been acceptable and more appropriate to their needs.

There are no facilities for young women facing custodial remands in Wales. If living in North Wales a young woman is likely to be sent to Risley Remand Centre in Liverpool and in South Wales to Eastwood Park in Gloucestershire.

In both instances the travelling times from the home area are likely to be long and expensive. As a result that young person is likely to receive less visits, increasing isolation and reducing the likelihood of repairing fractured family relationships and the opportunity to explore options like supported bail in the community.

All these factors indicate that rurality makes it difficult to provide equitable services, as the low number of young people in rural areas do not create the same demand as their urban counterparts. Providing mobile resources, outreach work and utilising existing community resources and networks are all strategies that need consideration.

Welsh Language Issues

Welsh identity is an increasingly important issue and this is in many respects manifested through the use of the Welsh language, "the Welsh language is more than an academic subject, it is the fountain of life" (Lord Gwilym Prys Davies, 1994).

Welsh is not a dying language, spoken by elderly rustics who populate the further reaches of Snowdownia, resisting any form of progress and defiantly burning down anything that appears to be remotely English.

You may be surprised to note that Welsh has more speakers now than it did 10 years ago. In rural North West Wales 61 per cent of the population are Welsh speakers, in West Wales 44 per cent of the population do so - for a significant proportion Welsh is the first language and many are monoglots but perhaps more surprisingly, an equally high proportionate use of Welsh is to be found in the urban and dare I say "perceptively English" concentrations in South Wales, including the capital Cardiff.

The Welsh Language Act was introduced in 1993 to promote the use of the Welsh language, in particular in the conduct of public business and the administration of justice in Wales. The English and Welsh languages should be treated equally.

The Act aims to ensure that services such as those provided by local authorities and the probation service can be provided in both English and Welsh. The Welsh Language Act clearly stands alongside other legislation that promotes anti-discriminatory practice. So why is this an important issue in our dealings with young people?

For young people moving into Welsh speaking areas, there is the challenge of learning and adapting to the language. Social life in these communities is predominantly Welsh and Welsh-speaking youth will have a far wider range of activities and pursuits in which to engage themselves. Very often these incoming young people may feel isolated and may not find out about Welsh language services and provision. Incomers need to learn the Welsh language to participate fully in education and local social life. Moving to a new area is disruptive and unsettling for a young person without the pressure of having to learn a new language. I do not want to present a stereotype, but marginalisation, boredom and discontent can be precursors to getting into trouble

What about those who speak Welsh as a first language? The Welsh language act requires local authorities and the probation service to develop Welsh language policies, setting out ways of developing Welsh services. They are no longer able to assume that they can operate mainly in English. They should have regard for the linguistic nature of Wales and either the monoglot or bilingual nature of the people they work with.

It is important to apply this to the services that are offered to young people - these are often youngsters with significant difficulties in their lives, who at best may find it difficult to communicate, and this becomes exacerbated when they are forced to express not what they need to express, but only what they can express because they are unable to use the language of their choice - in this instance Welsh.

This is particularly important when we think of the pre trial process for example - being detained in the police station, being interviewed about an alleged offence, being charged, transferred to local authority accommodation, appearing the next day in court, giving your name, etc. At the start of court proceedings and saying guilty or not guilty at the end while people talk about you and not to you. The process is confusing, possibly frightening because outcomes are uncertain, there are a whole range of different people involved and everything is going on in a language that they are not comfortable with. This scenario is not meeting young people's needs within the children act let alone the Welsh language act.

Young Welsh speaking people need to know that they can be dealt with in the language they are most comfortable with. Providing bilingual information that advertises this and explains processes and procedures is essential not just for young people but their families as well. Cardiff Social Services, for example, is currently producing a series of leaflets about what it means to be on remand and Ceredigion is drafting literature to explain the court process and procedures.

Gwynedd has a Welsh language policy which means that all young people are offered the Welsh language option, but that is not necessarily so in all the other Welsh authorities, which may rely on the availability of Welsh speaking team members rather than guarantee to provide that service. However, all parts of Wales have a right to expect the provision of services in the language of their choice.

Finally, issues around nationality and language also manifest themselves when young people, particularly from North Wales, are placed in custody in England, possibly in an establishment with a strong Mancunian/Liverpudlian culture. They stand out because of their language or their accents. This makes them vulnerable as they are isolated and many young people in such situations are victims of bullying and intimidation. A practitioner in North Wales recently told me that her team had been contacted by a governor of a young offender institution and the gist of the conversation had been that the young Welsh boy who was currently on remand there was not safe because of the intimidation he was being subjected to because of his nationality. When discussing rural issues I mentioned that the lack of local remand options contributes to this problem.

Local Government Re-organisation

The final issue I want to briefly cover is local government re-organisation in Wales.

Local Government re-organisation is perhaps an odd thing to talk about in relation to equality of provision but I feel that it is relevant because in some respects it has also exacerbated some of the issues raised earlier.

Prior to local government re-organisation in Wales in 1996 there were eight counties. There are now 22 local authorities which each provide a scaled down version of the full range of local services in respect of housing, education, transport and children's services.

The quality and nature of social work provision has been affected by this change. In a recent study of children's services plans 50 per cent of local authorities identified that local government re-organisation had a significant impact on service provision and, for a number, the ability to provide a quality service that meets a range of competing needs (NACRO, 1997). This is now significantly more difficult to achieve.

Financial constraints have dominated decision-making. For example, we have seen the loading of resources on to child protection services, with less priority given to other services such as youth justice. This has led to considerable tensions as local authorities have now been given lead responsibilities for developing structures for youth offending teams. Was it someone like Caius Patronious who said we regroup, restructure and re-organise but it never actually gets us anywhere. That is not quite right but the gist of it is there.

The introduction of youth offending teams will mean a further re-definition of boundaries and attendant losses and gains.

But what has some of this meant in practical terms? There is increased fragmentation and isolation of services particularly in rural areas. For example, prior to local government re-organisation North Wales was on the whole covered by two very good schemes offering mediation and reparation. Reparation is a key theme contained in the orders proposed under the Crime and Disorder Bill. Following re-organisation these projects have all but disappeared, existing in a much smaller capacity. These functions may be undertaken by social workers, who with competing demands on their time are increasingly less able to provide them. Services young people previously had access to are now no longer available and if we consider that one of the aims of reparation is to assist young people to think through the consequences of their actions and help them to prevent them re-offending, it is a significant loss.

Local re-organisation has also resulted in a loss of strategic direction. For example Dyfed had a joint probation and social services protocol which aimed to ensure that young people would be dealt with consistently across a wide ranging geographical area. This particularly related to court processes and procedures and responsibilities for 17 year olds. This agreement no longer exists which means that young people are not being dealt with as effectively as before, which can only be seen as a retrograde step.

Re-organisation of boundaries has also presented other difficulties, notably through the loss of provision. For example a number of new county borough councils have lost residential facilities, remand fostering schemes, volunteer support, etc. and what we most commonly see is where one area has lost out to another it can not afford to buy in.

This has been a cook's tour but I have briefly highlighted some of the factors that I feel I can confidently say most youth justice practitioner in Wales will echo.

Maintaining service provision is now a major preoccupation in Wales rather than improving and developing provision to ensure that young people's needs, no matter how diverse, are routinely and constructively addressed.

References

Lord Gwilym Prys Davies, speaking at *Securing a Quality Service in Wales – What about Linguistic Rights?* A Welsh conference for Social Workers, February 24th and 25th, 1994.

Nothing Ever Happens Around Here: Developing Youth Work with Young People in Rural Areas, National Youth Agency, Leicester, 1994.

Plans for Youth Justice – An Evaluation of the Youth Justice Element of Children's Services Plans in Wales, Youth Crime Section, NACRO, 1997.

PROGRAMMES FOR SERIOUS AND PERSISTENT OFFENDERS

Professor David Smith, University of Lancaster, England

Introduction

These observations arise specifically from my recent involvement in evaluating for The Scottish Office two projects for persistent juvenile offenders, and more generally from my interest over many years in trying to support creative, community-based responses to juvenile offending. The purpose of this short paper is to suggest what kinds of practice and organisation are associated with an approach to persistent juvenile offending which is positive, forward-looking and developmental, as opposed to negative, defensive and suspicious, and to outline some of what may be the crucial conditions for such an approach to survive in an intensive project for the most persistent juvenile offenders.

Essential Features of Socially Inclusive Practice with Young Offenders

There are good grounds for thinking that one of the reasons for the relative failure of most projects which attempt to reform offenders is that the positive elements of their work are outweighed or at least heavily compromised by the negative elements. That is, constructive changes, for example improvements in offenders' cognitive processes or social skills, are likely to be balanced by negative changes associated with stigmatic labelling and social exclusion. This is the crucial reason for the failure of most institutionally-based programmes, but it also applies to many programmes which are supposedly 'community-based', but are so only in the sense that the recipients of their services are not actually in custody or some other kind of institution.

One important aspect of a project committed to a socially inclusive approach to persistent offenders is, therefore, the extent to which it is genuinely embedded in supportive local networks which can enable access to mainstream resources in education, training, leisure and ultimately opportunities for employment. The classic 1980s' model of intermediate treatment in England and Wales, though not in Scotland, tended to isolate the specialist work from these networks and resources, through a deliberate concentration on offending behaviour to the exclusion of all else (as part of the reaction to what were rightly seen as the excesses and injustices of a naive 'welfare' approach to young offenders).

This suggests a second element of socially inclusive practice: that young people's offending should not be conceived in abstraction from other aspects of their lives, and in particular from the family experiences which will inevitably have been a powerful influence on their development. Experience shows that parents and other family members generally welcome opportunities for participation in the work of intensive projects: in all but a few cases, there is someone who cares, and can be helped to find ways of expressing that care practically and effectively. In giving family members and members of other social networks the chance of actively contributing to the effort to reduce young people's offending, workers may find, as is reported from Family Group Conferences in Australia, that they discover creative possibilities of protective incapacitation (which need not mean custody, as is often assumed) - for example, an elder brother may agree to take the young person to football matches on Saturday afternoons, or the local off-licence manager may agree not to serve him or her alcoholic drinks.

Thirdly, there is clear evidence that the quality of practice matters. Successful projects have committed staff who communicate care and respect, who can work flexibly rather than following a fixed curriculum, who can mix methods according to the young person's aptitudes and preferences (not everyone can cope with group work, for example), and who are allowed to work in an environment which provides the basic human needs of security and comfort. Everyone who has experience of day care or residential projects for young people in trouble will have come across many which fail on these criteria, and a few which succeed. The components of success are partly in the physical environment, but more importantly the style and approach of the workers. Successful projects have workers who can convey that they:

- are prepared to wait until the young person is ready to begin work

- have time to listen, that they accept young people with all their faults, that they can empathise without overwhelming them with their goodness (basically, the qualities identified over thirty years ago by Truax and Carkhuff as the most important for therapeutic success). These are certainly qualities of individual workers, but the capacity to maintain them is also a function of the working environment: projects need to be properly resourced, workers need to be securely employed, and managers need to be accessible and supportive, not remote and ready to blame.

Fourthly, and finally, in respect of practice and organisation, there is a good case for thinking that projects where attendance is voluntary are more likely to succeed than those where there is some element of compulsion (even if, as in the Scottish system, the sanctions available for non-compliance may appear unimpressive).

Attendance

From a south of the border perspective, one of the most astonishing aspects of one of the projects we have been evaluating is that there is no statutory basis at all for the young people's attendance (and no-one seems to think that there should be). Generally (nothing succeeds all the time with everyone), young people attend although, or because, there is no formal requirement that they should. They do so because they experience benefits from attending. All the research on the circumstances in which people are effectively helped to change suggests that they respond better when their co-operation is freely given, when, that is, they are able to identify with their helpers rather than seeing them as members of some other group.

Among the most interesting recent developments in social psychology is self-categorisation theory, which, in essence, claims that we all live with some set of groups in our heads, and that in different places and at different times we see ourselves as members of one or another of these groups. The Scottish Children's Hearing System probably does much better than a Youth Court in allowing young offenders to become members of the group of people who are worried about crime and want to do something positive about it; and so will a project which is based on enlisting young people's active co-operation rather than their fearful agreement.

Elements for a Successful Project

If these four conditions of creative and positive practice are present in a project, what does it need to survive and prosper? Fundamentally, it needs to be supported by a broad local consensus that it is worth supporting. This means that, unlike most such projects, it should be one part - the most obvious and visible part - of a local strategy on young offenders and young people at risk. There are parallels here with the contrasts drawn by Michael King and John Pitts between British and French approaches to crime prevention in the 1980s and early 1990s - the former 'project-driven', short-term and 'implanted' into local communities, the latter 'programme-driven', expected to produce results over several years and not within months, and based on local inter-agency and political support.

The most often repeated message when we began to evaluate the Freagarrach Project, based in Alloa and Falkirk, was that it was the 'tip of the iceberg' - that is, it was underpinned by a much larger inter-agency strategy on young offenders. This strategy has had to survive local government reorganisation, but generally speaking it has done so. The credit for originating the strategy belongs to the police; but it was quickly and actively supported by the Education Department, the Reporters to the Children's Hearings, the Social Work Department, and Barnardo's, which runs the project. The strategy has recently been reworked to reflect the changed conditions since the changes in local government, but the essence of its original formulation remains intact.

Evaluation of the Project

In summary, this means that the police will, whenever possible, respond informally to minor offending by juveniles, not by doing nothing, but by encouraging them into available sports and leisure facilities; and, crucially, they will give the project leader access to their computer database on offending by young people, so that she can be sure that the project retains a clear focus on its target group and, when necessary, actively seek referrals from social workers. The Education Department made a commitment, which has survived disaggregation, to provide places in day units for young people attending the project, and to work co-operatively on reintegration into mainstream education. An anti-exclusion strategy has also survived, though it is now unevenly implemented across the three new authorities; but the innovation of seconding teachers to the Reporter's office, to provide a quick response to school-related problems, proved vulnerable to the immediate fiscal pressures on small local authorities. The Reporters, however, have maintained their support for the principle of voluntary attendance at the project, and have consistently diverted young people at Freagarrach from formal hearings when they have re-offended.

The Social Work Department's main contribution was probably the secondment of staff to the project, which has also survived reorganisation; and at the level of individual practice, social workers have consistently kept faith and believed in the project, allowed it to do its work, and generally avoided making inappropriate referrals. Other supportive networks have included voluntary sector organisations concerned with alcohol and drugs misuse, links with colleges and local employers, and, since October 1997, with the Apex Forth Valley Project, which aims to prepare marginalised young people for participation in the labour market. It has already proved a valuable resource for young people leaving Freagarrach. Unfortunately funding for the Apex Project is due to come to an end by the end of March 1999.

In Conclusion

All conclusions are tentative. Mine, on the basis of this research, is that community-based projects for young offenders are most likely to succeed when they meet the conditions I have outlined. The corollary applies: they are least likely to succeed when they do not. But the point I made at the beginning still applies: the best of projects still have to compensate for the potentially negative effects of stigmatisation and exclusion. They also have a basic social obligation to show that they are doing something useful.

In becoming more closely acquainted with the Children's Hearing System I was most immediately struck by its virtues compared with the Youth Court south of the border: it allows for dialogue, participation, and the expression of care. But too often it does nothing. When young people at the projects I have been evaluating re-offend, the most usual response of the Reporter is 'no further action': the young person is already receiving as much care and attention as we can give, and nothing more can be done. But the system is in fact ideally suited to do what should be done in such cases: to respond actively to the renewed offending, but not in a way which rejects the young person as a person. This idea comes from what I consider the most creative and practically relevant development in criminology in the last ten years: John Braithwaite's theory of re-integrative shaming. This says, in very summary form, that ignoring crime makes things worse, that responding to crime in stigmatising ways makes things worse still, and that responding to crime in ways that convey disapproval of the act while retaining an attitude of respect to the offender may make things better. Obviously there are resource implications here, which I cannot discuss now, but the Children's Hearing System looks like a ready-made mechanism for conveying disapproval of the offence without out-casting the offender. Maybe it should use this power more often?

YOUNG PEOPLE IN CUSTODY - A TIME FOR CHANGE

Tony Kavanagh, Northern Ireland Office, Northern Ireland

Introduction

Care and Control

While the debate continues on the relative merits of the justice and welfare approaches to juvenile offenders (with justice ahead in most jurisdictions, but with Scotland as a notable exception) few now see the answer lying at either poles of the argument. Several commentators point to the now most common response to disillusionment with either approach, as the development of a juvenile justice system which uses dual or mixed philosophies and practices. Such proposals, they point out, commonly aim to divert juveniles from the formal system where possible, but where formal action is justified, then elements of due process, justice and welfare are combined. The Black Report is often cited as recommending this approach.

Taken as an overall package, including the legal framework and the clearly stated policy intentions, Northern Ireland is now moving to this compromise position with custody, the bastion of the justice or control camps, set to become the least significant element in an altogether more sophisticated approach to juvenile offending. Greater emphasis will be placed on prevention and diversion, with restorative justice also providing a locus for the victim and the community at large. Over time the balance of expenditure will shift from custody to supporting community-based disposals. The full implementation of the Children (NI) Order 1995 and the development of Children's Services Plans will be an integral part of this strategy.

Nevertheless, custody will still be required as a disposal of last resort for at least some juveniles who commit serious offences or who are seriously persistent in their offending.
The principles that will guide the approach to custody are well supported (at least in justice circles and probably beyond) and present an irresistible case for how we in Northern Ireland should proceed. The principles are contained in five self-explanatory, if somewhat clumsy, words and are as follows:

- Determinacy
- Proportionality
- Equity
- Specificity
- Frugality

Perhaps the best way to describe their meaning is to test them against the current system and the arrangements under the new Criminal Justice (Children) Order.

Determinacy

The current system, based on the Children and Young Persons Act 1968, does not provide for determinate sentencing; we euphemistically refer to the Training School Order (TSO) as semi-determinate but, in reality and in relation to the life of a child, it is as long as a piece of string.

Proportionality

Nor is the TSO proportionate to the offence for which it has been given; we routinely see the same custodial order awarded for offences ranging from the pettiest of thefts to violent assault with actual duration determined in most instances by factors unrelated to the original offence.

Equity

Similarly, equity is in short measure since a period in custody will be determined by external factors such as family background, access to education and, because of the wide discretion given to managers, the Training School the young offender happens to be in. If he (the Training School population is overwhelmingly male) is from a good home background and can return to full-time education, stays can be relatively short. If on the other hand, he comes from a care background and cannot be reintegrated into school, then he might expect to stay in the justice system considerably longer. It is also important to note that the TSO takes no account of remand time thus introducing further inequity into the system.

Specificity

The TSO also fails on the specificity test. When a child is committed to a Training School, he or she has no way of knowing when they will be released against a background of arcane practices in relation to home leave, extended leave and recall from license for reasons unconnected with offending. The system encourages a leisurely approach to custody with the evident feeling that with up to two years to play with, there is no need to set short-term targets for release back into the community.

Frugality

Finally, we are still not very sparing or frugal with the use of custody. While the Criminal Justice (NI) Order 1996 will filter out many of the petty offenders we still retain children in custody for far too long because, again, the system encourages it. The TSO places too much discretion in the hands of the professionals, institutionalises the children and fails to properly engage other statutory agencies in providing appropriate support arrangements in the community. It is, in every respect, corrosive of children's rights. This is also evident in the high levels of remand in secure custody, a most paradoxical state of affairs as, on a finding of guilt, children are transferred to the "open" setting on the basis of religion.

A Time for Change

When we apply the test to the proposed Criminal Justice (Children) (NI) Order, the outcome is somewhat different. Significantly, it is determinate and everyone will know and will be able to prepare for the time when the child is to be released. Within the rules governing the minimum and standard sentence of 6 months (a sufficient period of time set to allow for some practical work to be done and to avoid short, sharp shocks), a magistrate has more scope to align offence and sentence, thus introducing a much needed element of proportionality and flexibility. The equity condition is met by allowing the courts to determine length of stay based on offence and by taking account of remand time. Other factors, which are properly outside the remit and control of the justice system, will no longer be allowed to influence duration of sentence and return to custody will only be through the courts.

The new custodial juvenile justice centre order will also be quite specific in its terms. The date of release from custody will be fixed as will the duration of the community element of the sentence. By working within these fixed parameters, the intention will be to develop a much more structured and positive regime geared to adding value in terms of education, life and cognitive skills and the capacity to thrive, not in the artificial and dependence-inducing atmosphere of custody, but in the community. Lastly there is a clear intention that custody should be used with increasing frugality with the ultimate, though unachievable, aim of having no one in custody at all. By definition, though, most of those who do find their way into custody will be held securely because their offending will be at the serious end of the spectrum and public protection will be an important consideration. Furthermore, the new Order will place restrictions on the use of custodial remands by imposing a presumption of bail in almost all but the most serious and persistent cases.

That custody for some young offenders is necessary as a means of protecting society in undeniable. Equally undeniable is that custody is a process that can damage young people who are already significantly disadvantaged in a whole series of ways - it is not, by and large, an influence for the good despite the best efforts of some very committed people who work in the system. Indeed, at a time when social inclusion is being promoted as a concept, custody represents the most extreme form of state-sponsored social exclusion available. It appears to add little value yet absorbs vast quantities of resources. Notwithstanding the various international conventions, its use should be minimised for the entirely pragmatic reason that it does not work very well.

What we put in its place is a subject in its own right but as a broad generalisation I would argue that rather than looking for alternatives to custody we should be looking for alternative strategies to the use of custody. While interventions in the form of progressively stiffer penalties will be a continued requirement - though more imagination could be applied here - prevention and early intervention, and sustaining the young person in the community through effective inter-agency partnerships, are the real keys to success and have been identified as such by the Audit Commission (Misspent Youth), in the Riyadh Guidelines and the very progressive, for its time, Black Report; but most striking of all and still true today are the words of the 19th century reformer, Mary Carpenter:

"...those who have not yet fallen into actual crime but who are almost certain, from their destitution and the circumstances in which they are growing up to do so, if a helping hand be not extended to raise them".

The grasp of the juvenile justice system on those who enter custody is very tight indeed. In Northern Ireland, at least, we must make sure that that does not continue to be the reality.

PROGRAMMES FOR SERIOUS AND PERSISTENT OFFENDERS

Rob Allen, Director of Research and Development, NACRO, England

Introduction

There seems a growing sense of pessimism in England and Wales about serious and persistent young offenders. At a recent large inter-agency conference on the Crime and Disorder Bill, a participant said that he felt that it was a waste of effort and resource to try to change the behaviour of 14, 15 and 16 year olds. Rather than use expensive secure accommodation or construct elaborate community programmes, he felt it much better for incorrigible teenagers to go to prison and to use the money saved to help the parents of younger children, thus preventing a future generation of serious or persistent offenders. This was not a police officer or a magistrate talking, but a senior manager from the Social Services Department. In similar vein last week, at a meeting to discuss the role of health professionals in the forthcoming youth offending teams in England and Wales, a consultant psychiatrist said that such was the premium on evidence-based practice and on treating the most treatable patients, that it would be difficult to prioritise unpromising delinquents who show little signs of wanting to change. Further, a respected criminologist and crime prevention guru, Ken Pease, recently told the Home Affairs Select Committee inquiry on alternatives to prison, that in his view the prison population should be some 30,000 higher than it currently is. In his view community supervision simply did not protect the public adequately from persistent offenders. Although he was giving evidence alongside two maverick former probation officers, who reckoned the prison population should be about 300,000 rather than the 65,000 it currently stands at, and therefore Ken's position was, relatively speaking, a moderate one, there seems a growing consensus emerging from the community safety agenda that incarceration has an important part to play in preventing and reducing crime.

The air of pessimism about serious and persistent young offenders contrasts with an air of optimism around the promise of early intervention with children at risk and about restorative justice, which have been looked at already. The aim of this paper is to say a little about what we know of serious and persistent young offenders and implications for programmes we might wish to develop.

Characteristics of Persistent Young Offenders

Later this year, we are launching a report called 'Wasted Lives', which describes the life histories, backgrounds and experiences of 40 boys in young offender institutions in England and Wales. The in-depth interviews with the boys, almost all of whom were serious and persistent offenders, makes depressing reading. Well over half saw home as less than supportive, with many describing sometimes quite severe levels of violence at home. All but three of the 40 had either been expelled for persistent truancy, or simply left school. One in four claimed to have taken hard drugs, with well over half users of cannabis. Violence at home, at school and indeed in the young offender institutions was seen as being an accepted part of their lives.

The findings mirror, to a large extent, other research by Gwyneth Boswell, into the characteristics of Section 53 offenders, and by Ann Hagell and Tim Newburn into persistent offenders. The first found very high levels of abuse, neglect and traumatic loss in the lives of children convicted of very serious crimes, including very high rates of sexual abuse. The latter found chaotic family situations and, sometimes, intensive involvement with social services departments. What all the research has shown is that these groups of youngsters have very high levels of need. While these are in no way excuses for their behaviour, they are clearly factors which need to be tackled if we are serious about trying to reverse the direction of these young lives. The question is how to tackle them.

Prevention through Early Intervention

The first way of course, is prevention. I visited two interesting American programmes during a Winston Churchill Travelling Fellowship last year. The Quantum Opportunities Programme (QOP) is an intensive four-year educational enhancement programme for 25 at risk youths from inner city Philadelphia. Youngsters are randomly selected from ninth grade and are expected to take 250 hours of education, 250 of service to the community, 250 of development each year for four years. The education consists of a specially developed computer assisted learning programme. Each youngster is allocated to a counsellor who acts as a mentor. Perhaps the most interesting aspect is the fact that financial incentives are offered to participants. They are paid an hourly stipend ($1 an hour rising to $1.33) and after completion of 100 hours of participation receive $100 bonus. At this point whatever stipends are earned are matched by contributions to an accrual account which can be used by participants only if and when they graduate from high school and only for educational purposes.

The philosophy of the programme is a no nonsense tough love approach. Children must dress smartly and lose eligibility for stipends if they swear, goof around or even bring in food. On the other hand the commitment of the staff is truly inspiring: 24 hours a day, year round availability. Results of the programme are impressive. 63% of youngsters involved in QOP graduate from school compared to 42% of the control group. Only 23% drop out compared to 50%, 24% of the QOP group become teen parents compared to 38% of the controls and while the arrest rate for controls is 0.58 per person during the juvenile years the figure for the QOP group is 0.17.

The Rand Corporation have compared the crime preventive effect of graduation incentive programmes, such as QOP, with other kinds of intervention and concluded that compared to home visits and day care, parent training, delinquent supervision and three strikes and you're out policies, graduation incentives prevent more serious crimes per million dollars. Rand also calculated that the criminal justice system's savings from graduation incentives are a substantial fraction of programme costs. In the case of QOP the programme pays for itself.

There are a number of important lessons from the success of the programme. First and foremost youngsters who will often be written off will take advantage of opportunities like these which are put their way. Continuity is important. Long term investment in children and the creation of longstanding relationships can go some way to compensating for some of the early damage which is sustained in childhood. Money matters too and the incentives provided both by the stipends and the accrual account seem to be important. As important as cash in hand is the notion that someone is investing in these children on a large scale. That may be the most significant factor for social policy.

The second programme, is the "8% Solution". This programme is a highly targeted intervention aimed at youngsters who are likely to become persistent or chronic offenders. The probation service in Orange County undertook a detailed study of young people who were referred to them. They discovered that about 70% did not come to their notice again, 21% had two or three other contacts while 8% of youngsters came back four or more times. The 8% were responsible for more than half of the repeat offences committed. By studying a sample of files the probation services were able to identify four factors which were strongly associated with the 8%.

- A school behaviour or performance factor which consists of chronic attendance problems, and/or behaviour problems, and/or poor grades
- A Family problem factor which comprises poor parental supervision and control, significant family problems, criminal family members exerting negative influence on the child, or documented child abuse or neglect
- A substance abuse factor which includes the use of alcohol or drugs in any way but experimentation
- A delinquency factor, which means early onset of stealing behaviour, running away or becoming a member of a gang

Having identified these characteristics the probation service decided to try to intervene early with young people who displayed them at the time of their first contact in order to prevent them becoming chronic offenders. They have developed a long term, multidisciplinary approach to these children, providing an 18 month intensive programme. Children are picked up from home at 7.30 and taken to a youth and family resource centre where they receive four hours education followed by a programme of recreation and skill building. There is intensive work with families via in-home services providing assistance with budgeting and home making skills. The programme includes a $10,000 discretionary fund to help the families of 8%ers also undertake a programme of community service to build-up a stake in the local neighbourhood.

The probation service has found considerable support for the initiative from other agencies. Paediatricians for example became very interested in what is a highly targeted approach which offers the promise of reductions in emergency room admissions, school failures and a whole host of other social disadvantages as well as reductions in crime. The original 8% programme does seem to have had success. While 86% of the original 8% study group had a subsequent commitment to an institution the proportion of the field test group receiving the intensive services was only 43%. Since January 1997 a random experimental design has been in operation which should provide more evidence of the effectiveness of this approach.

In neighbouring Los Angeles County the approach has been taken one step further, by a multi-agency at risk youth committee, (known as Maary-C). Rather than wait until an offender's first contact with the probation service, the aim of the initiative in Los Angeles is to identify those youngsters most likely to become chronic offenders before they offend. In a pilot project covering four zip codes in Long Beach, school teachers are asked to identify youngsters who display the characteristics associated with persistency. In the case of Los Angeles the persistent group accounts for 16% rather than 8% of the total proportion of offenders.

Critical Programme Elements for Successful Intervention

As far as the 8% early intervention programme is concerned, there are sixteen critical programme elements: –

1. Focus on the correct target population.

2. Work with entire family unit i.e. all who live in home.

3. Provide a "Balanced Approach" of supportive interventions, offender accountability and offender risk control activities.

The "Balanced Approach" assists juvenile justice programmes in prescribing clear outcomes directed at the three primary "clients": juvenile offenders, victims and the community, and measuring the results in terms of specific improvements in offender competency, victim restoration and community protection.

4. Acquisition of a programme site (Youth & Family Resource Centre) accessible within the target area, capable of housing all key programme staff and co-ordinating service delivery.

5. Experienced probation officers to provide case management services for the probationer and his/her family. (Caseloads should generally not exceed 15 cases per officer as they will have an average of 4 additional family members per case that they will be working with.).

6. Comprehensive assessment of the juvenile probationer and all family members, to identify strengths and factors contributing to offence behaviour.
Every effort will be made to identify and capitalise on each family member's strengths and to reduce the negative impact of contributing risk factors. Educational and medical assessment and follow-up on identified problems will be critical to the long-term success of such early intervention efforts.
During the pilot project, the local chapter of the American Academy of Paediatrics conducted assessments of 8% minors in the field test programme and their siblings. A high proportion of 8% minors will have undiagnosed and untreated learning disabilities, mental health problems such as clinical depression and post traumatic stress syndrome and other medical problems contributing to delinquency.

7. Intensive in-home family intervention/support services and associated parent education and support groups co-ordinated with all other programme elements.

8. Substance abuse counselling services for both minors and adults.

9. Some discretionary funds to meet special (or crisis) needs of minors and their families.

10.A community service component which involves individual and group activities of a restorative nature to both the probationer and the community. This allows the minor to make amends which builds self-esteem while providing any victims and the community with a tangible programme benefit.

11.Programme components to assist 8% youth and families to develop skills that enable them to move from dependency to competency. This must include both cognitive and action components where juveniles and adults have many opportunities to practice the new skills being learned.

12.Each minor's programme must be individualised, provide sufficient structure and be of sufficient intensity to achieve and reinforce positive behaviour change. (This is true for the parents and siblings of 8% youth as well).

13.The provision of transportation for minors and family members is critical to ensure consistent access to and full participation in key programme activities.

14.Frequent contact and consultation with the minor's parents, teachers and other community-based organisations participating in the minor's and family's intervention programme.

15.Extensive use of volunteers and community resources to enhance the programme and increase programme intensity.

16.Maintenance of detailed documentation on each minor/family's progress for programme evaluation and feedback to operations.

These elements, whilst designed for an early intervention approach, are relevant not only to nipping offending in the bud, but as part of a programme later on in a young offender's career.

Moving back to England and Wales, there is no doubt that there is an important culture change in youth justice at the moment. A move from the three D's of diversion from crime, diversion from prosecution and diversion from custody to the three R's of responsibility, restoration and reintegration, means a move from an emphasis on keeping people out of the system to getting them into it. One consequence is a renewed focus on what you actually do with young offenders. The Audit Commission has called for a lot more work to be done on tackling offending behaviour and there has been a range of publications by the Institute for the Study and Treatment of Delinquency, the Probation Inspectorate and various other organisations, suggesting particular programmes. In fact the port-folio of tried and tested programmes is relatively thin and in the current context there is a growing market in nicely packaged interventions, whether they are protective behaviours, solution focussed therapy or cognitive restructuring. There are nicely packaged organisations to provide them as well. There is nothing new in this. In the 1980s a lot of intensive intermediate programmes used the "correctional curriculum" developed by David Smith and his colleagues at Lancaster University. Such programmes have two distinct advantages. They bring focus to efforts to working with young offenders and they add intensity.

Outstanding Problems

The Audit Commission's finding that youngsters on supervision receive only about an hour a week of face to face contact, suggests the need for a good deal more intensity if youngsters are to be helped out of a delinquent lifestyle. Intensity and structure in the criminal justice context will, however, bring its own problems with more failures and more breaches. A review of American research on intensive probation programmes has found rather disappointing evidence in respect of recidivism rates and high levels of young people entering custody by the back door of breach rather than the front door of custodial sentences. As they stand, the national standards in England and Wales for supervision orders, with their requirements for regular reporting, prompt commencement and so on, stand in stark contrast to the characteristics of persistent young offenders described by researchers. What is clearly needed is flexible out-reach programmes, which can bring back severely disaffected youngsters into mainstream activities.

A further problem concerns the tendency of programmes being based on "doing things to people". The development of technical programmes with the need for programme integrity ignores the fact that for many young offenders developing and sustaining a relationship with a decent adult in their lives is probably the most important vehicle to getting straightened out.

A final problem arises from the fragmentation of approaches to young people, particularly where offence specific programmes have been developed. There is a danger that different elements in peoples' lives are increasingly taken in isolation. The US evidence very much suggests that multi-modal approaches work the best, which suggests that a flexible variety of methods are needed.

So what are the lessons?

Effective measures in the community are in many ways the key to a successful response to offending by young people. Three steps suggest themselves as ways to improve their success.

First, research is beginning to identify the kinds of measures which are most effective in reducing offending behaviour in adults. Intensive structured programmes consisting of several contacts a week which focus on getting offenders to think before they act show particular promise. There is a need to tailor such cognitive approaches to children and to recognise the limited attention span, "hard-to-reach" character and chaotic lifestyle of many teenage offenders. Many of the most difficult offenders will have experienced adults giving up on them in various ways from an early age –

particularly at home and at school. The more persistent the offending, the more persistent are the efforts needed to curb it.

Second, there is scope for greater involvement of families in the process of supervision. The Cambridge University evaluation of intermediate treatment found that parents were seldom invited to participate in the programme and would have welcomed that opportunity. Research has shown that including families in the treatment plans for the most disturbed and difficult children in institutional care is a key to a successful outcome. There is every reason to suppose that improved family functioning and parent-child relations should be important aims for interventions all through the system. There is particular excitement in the possibilities of Family Group Conferencing as a way of doing this.

Third, there is a need for community-based supervision to utilise as wide a range of resources as possible in the task of promoting responsibility. Too high a burden of expectation currently falls on the shoulders of individual social workers or probation officers. Their efforts are more likely to bear fruit if undertaken in partnership with other agencies, organisations and individuals in the local community. Schools, youth clubs, churches, voluntary organisations and employers need to accept a greater measure of responsibility for the life of the community as a whole and for offering opportunities to reintegrate young people excluded from it. There are questions of culture and attitude as well as practicality here. There is a trend towards a more punitive approach to offenders in general and the press coverage of young offenders given "holidays" has eroded confidence in community supervision. There are, however, areas where co-operation and co-ordination of services and resources are good and where innovative practice thrives. While hard, objective evidence of effectiveness is limited, schemes which combine elements of education, basic and social skills training and work, and which make use of mentors – adult volunteers who act as advisors and friends – show promise for disaffected teenagers.

WHAT WORKS WITH JUVENILE OFFENDERS?

Michael E. O'Connor, Oberstown House, Ireland

Introduction

What are juvenile offenders? It is difficult to define exactly what is meant by the term, other than to conclude that they are 'juveniles that commit crimes'.

In recent years the subject of juvenile crime has received widespread and increasing attention. The public perception is that crime by young persons is not only on the increase, but is more serious than ever before (Pearson, 1983). This view is reflected by the Select Committee on Crime set up by the Irish Government in 1992:

> *"Youthful crime causes harm and hurt to the victim, the community and to the young people themselves. In addition, the risk of the youngsters in trouble developing into hardened adult criminals is very real....The Committee is particularly concerned about reports of even younger offenders coming to the attention of the authorities, for what may sometimes be quite serious incidents"* (Government Publication of Ireland, 1992).

This First Report of the Select committee on Crime (1992), which looked at juvenile crime, its causes and remedies, outlined that on average 3,500 young people under the age of 17 years were convicted of offences during the years 1987 to1990. Those aged between 14 and 17 years comprised of 17 per cent of all persons convicted during this period (Bates, 1996).

According to the Garda Síochána Crime Bureau in 1995, the most frequently committed crime by 14 to 17 year olds in 1994 was larceny from people, shops and motor vehicles (31.2%), with burglary (14.1%) and criminal damage next (12.8%), followed by car related offences (11%), drink and drug related offences (6.7%) and public order offences (4.2%) (Bates, 1996).

It is accepted that as different countries conceptualise juvenile offending in different ways, and their systems of juvenile justice differ, it is very difficult to formulate exact figures for comparative analysis (Junger-Tas, 1994). This said, it is possible to identify trends in Western Europe. Such trends include:

- most crimes are less serious property offences
- the number of offences grow faster than demographic rates
- most crimes are committed close to the offender's home
- there is an increase in offences involving violence, especially amongst males
- more girls are becoming involved in crime
- younger offenders are more involved in less serious property offences
- in many countries there is a disproportionate level of 'non-national' offending
- there is an increase in crime related to drug misuse.

(Bailleau, 1996).

Approaches to Dealing with Juvenile Offending

Armed with this understanding of juvenile offending and the extent of the offending, let me begin to address the question of 'What works ?'. What works is a 'sound byte' - like the 'Nothing works' school of the 1970s which acted as a powerful depressant and dealt the notion of the rehabilitation of offenders a severe blow. It proved to be a serious inhibitor to activities, but was not, and never has been, true. The phrase was simply a media sound byte (Smith, 1994).

There is much literature advocating the stance that 'nothing works' (Martinson, 1974). However, it is also argued that the evaluation of effectiveness involves factors other than recidivism (Macdonald, 1993). Interestingly, where controlled studies have been undertaken of correctional services, between 40 per cent and 80 per cent have reported some evidence of positive effect of service, in terms of re-offending, at least to a mild degree (Lipsey, 1989 and Palmer, 1992).

These findings are facilitated by **meta-analysis**. Meta-analysis is a statistical means of reviewing outcome literature which codes process and outcome characteristics described in the research (Corrado, 1992). Meta-analysis has contributed to a counter discourse within which **'what works ... with who'** is beginning to be identified. Literature reviews will show that, in the area of regime design, clinically relevant programmes that target specific factors in a young person's treatment history are most beneficial. Such regimes should be related to the causes of crime, as recommended by a psychologist, a psychiatrist, or other therapist. The literature highlights that what is essential, in terms of effectiveness, is 'best fit', or clinical relevance. This is in fact a 'contingency model' tailored to meet the needs of the young person. It is, I believe, the way forward. 'What works - with who' is a central **Modern** criminological question.

Care Programmes – Oberstown Boys Centre: A case in point

I shall now attempt to steer a path through the 'care programmes' that are offered to youngsters in the care of Oberstown Boys Centre, of which I am the Director. I, of course, subscribe to the school of thought that argues that 'prevention is better than cure'. It would be preferable if it were possible for Oberstown Boys Centre to deal exclusively with young offenders who are exhibiting challenging behaviour and those that are marginalised in our society. Unfortunately this is not the case.

We are licensed to accept boys between the ages of twelve and sixteen years, on admission. All of the boys are sentenced by the courts for a minimum period of two years. This has the effect of producing an average age profile in the Centre of sixteen to seventeen years. In terms of addressing the question of 'what works with who' in the context of juvenile offenders in a custodial setting, it must be understood that I am dealing with the older end of the juvenile market.

In order to further contextualise the Oberstown Boys Centre, I should state that we are an 'open Reformatory School' under the terms of the Children Act 1908 (very similar to the old Community Homes with Education that were prevalent in the U.K. in the early seventies).

Because we are 'open', without high walls and security staff, security is achieved through a combination of physical and human resources (Stewart & Tutt, 1987).

The 1996 Children Bill, presently at Committee stage in the House, will replace the 1908 Act. It is expected that the Bill will be enacted by the Irish Parliament towards the end of this year. Whilst the new legislation will bring many welcome changes to the way that youngsters who come into contact with the law will be dealt with, it will not, to any marked degree, alter the types and content of the care/rehabilitative programmes that are offered to the youngsters in Oberstown Boys Centre. Oberstown Boys Centre will still operate roughly mid way on a continuum of custodial provision for boys. At one end of this continuum are the 'Industrial Schools' which cater for the younger, less serious offender while at the other end is a secure facility which caters for a similar age range as those in Oberstown Boys Centre. Boys sentenced to the secure facility are those who have been convicted of the most serious crimes or those who are persistent absconders from the open Centre. There is also a facility to transfer boys, by Ministerial Order, from the open to the secure facility on grounds of persistent extreme assaultive behaviour.

As stated earlier, the causes of juvenile delinquency are multi-faceted and so too is the approach to dealing with these youngsters. Care programmes are designed to reflect a 'partnership' element between the carer and the client. This aspect affirms attitudes of empowerment, choice, rights, respect and relationships, rather than authority, powerlessness, punishment and subordination. Care programmes in Oberstown Boys Centre have four dimensions which seek to affirm the premise that the boys (clients) have needs in the Centre and outside of the Centre, and that success is not possible if we concentrate only on what goes on **in** the Centre. (See appendix 1)

Our care programmes are designed to bring about a change in the lives of the youngsters in our care. These care programmes work by (a) identifying needs (b) meeting those needs (c) the teaching of skills i.e. social, emotional, practical (d) changing attitudes (cognitive and moral development) which in turn facilitates (e) changes in behaviour, i.e. offending.

The four dimensions of care plans in Oberstown Boys Centre are:
- Primary Care (Teeth, clothes, food, shelter etc.).
- The Living Environment (Behaviour, Aggression, coping in the peer group etc.).
- Personal Development (Social Skills, Education, Personal issues, Anger Control, Self-esteem, Offending behaviour issues - this is the area of counselling and therapy).
- Outreach (Home leave, Trips out of the Centre, Work Programmes, Community Links and Aftercare)(Wall, 1997).

Ideally all boys sentenced to a period of detention in Oberstown Boys Centre, or indeed any Industrial or Reformatory School, should have been formally assessed to assist the Court to determine their needs, and to assist in appropriate sentencing (Kennedy Report to the Government 1970). This is in the main, what occurs, with some exceptions. However we have found that in very many cases the presenting boys were assessed in St Michael's Remand and Assessment Centre some twelve months to three years earlier. Obviously for an assessment to be of use it must be accurate and pertinent to the situation at the time. To this end, the Oberstown Boys Centre undertakes its own assessment on all boys sentenced to this disposal. This 'in house assessment' is crucial in terms of targeting specific factors in the young person's history to obtain the 'best fit' as mentioned earlier in relation to meta - analysis.

Initially the period of assessment (about eight weeks) is required in order to identify the strengths and weaknesses in the boy's character. This also serves to provide a 'benchmark' from which to measure any future progress. During this period the boy's educational ability, his social skills, his capacity to build relationships and his ability to adapt to group living, are all closely monitored.

Whilst this period of assessment is in progress the boy's 'key-worker' (a residential care staff member who has been allocated specific responsibility for that boy, in addition to his/her normal duties) will make contact with the boy's parents. Parents are encouraged to visit the Centre during the waking day, without restriction. The keyworker will, during the period of assessment, visit the parents in the home in an effort to assess the viability of the home situation and to foster positive relationships between the family and the professionals in the Centre.

The key-worker will also liase with the Probation and Welfare Officer and the Social Worker who have been allocated to that case. A comprehensive assessment of the family and the dynamics within that family is produced and at the end of the period of assessment a case conference is convened where all the interested parties are represented. It is at this case conference that the intervention plan for the boy is identified and detailed. As no two juveniles are exactly the same, neither are the 'care plans' for any two juveniles exactly the same. It is the individual nature of these care plans, tailored to address the needs of the individual child, that increase the likelihood of the intervention being successful.

It will not come as any great surprise to this audience, for me to state that almost all of the youngsters referred to Oberstown Boys Centre have a low self-esteem. It therefore appears that this is an appropriate place to begin the rehabilitative process. How can one expect a juvenile to have respect for property or for the feelings of others, if that juvenile does not have respect for himself?

We increase the self-esteem or self-opinion of the youngsters by participation in a series of individually designed programmes and by encouraging positive relationships with the adults in their environment. These individual programmes are centred on areas such as 'offending behaviour, social skills, substance abuse, sexuality, family, specifically focused counselling and psychological and/or psychiatric treatment/therapy where deemed necessary.

Group work and individual work are both used in the Centre. All of the boys attend the Education Centre (school). Almost all of the pupils sit the Junior Certificate (roughly equivalent to GCSE's). For many, obtaining pass grades or better is a magnificent achievement. Sometimes they are the first members of their families to gain a state certificate in an examination - albeit at foundation level.

'Workplace' skills is an area that is also very important to these youngsters if they are to take their place as productive members of society. To this end a number of the classes in the Education Centre are practical classes such as woodwork, home economics, art/crafts, computers, horticulture etc. For the academic year 1998/99 we hope to be able to provide building construction classes, motorcar and motorcycle mechanics classes and an expanded horticultural class.

Continued Re-offending

It would appear therefore, that we are offering a comprehensive service, in small group living situations (maximum of 10 boys per house) for juvenile offenders in a pleasant rural setting. Why then do these boys re-offend? Why do some of them offend whilst in Oberstown, whilst on home leave or even immediately on discharge?

Of course there is no one comprehensive answer. However, it would appear that at least part of the answer to the question of recidivism may rest with the parents. An integral part of any care programme (with elements of rehabilitation) especially in the case of children, must include a home leave programme. This home leave programme begins with a supervised home visit (supervised by the boy's key-worker). It then progresses to a 'dropped at home and picked up' day visit, dropped at home and picked up overnight visit and finally progressing to a weekend home leave schedule towards the end of the youngster's time with us.

Many years ago we discovered that while parents made appropriate comments to staff and to their children whilst on visits to the Centre and indeed when staff visited them in their homes, once the staff were not around many parents colluded with their children, ignored their children or were terrified of their children. In order to address this difficulty all parents are actively encouraged to attend the Parenting Group. This group meeting takes place on a monthly basis in a city centre location. It is run jointly by Probation and Welfare and the key-workers. Amongst the topics covered in this group are 'positive parenting skills', 'how to say 'no' to your child', 'drug education', 'budgetary skills', 'social welfare services', 'relationships' and 'health and hygiene'. The importance of the Parenting group cannot be overstated.

Other factors which may negatively affect the developmental progress of the young person whilst in custody can vary from living within a hostile group, (incidentally not always the case) to opportunistic absconding, to fear of bullying or intimidation, to degree of maturity of the youngster. It would appear therefore, that attempting to steer a path through this jungle is fraught with difficulties - and I would tend to agree. Where the human element is involved accurate predictions should be avoided!

So are we wasting our time and a lot of our taxpayers' money in the process? Certainly one could argue that, in short term gains, it would appear that any changes in the behaviours/characters of the youngsters are minor and possibly short-lived. I take the opposite view, I feel that success cannot be measured in short-term gains. It is the synergy created by the experience of spending two years in Oberstown Boys Centre that will equip the youngster to deal with the difficulties that he will face later in life. These youngsters are still developing and are impressionable. They are not yet capable of taking charge of their own lives. We teach them skills to empower them to deal with the challenges that they will face in the future.

Unfortunately it may be two or three years after they have left Oberstown that they begin to examine their lives, as mature young adults. It is this maturation process that is so important in determining success. Because they will have been equipped with skills such as education, social skills, employment skills, relationship building skills etc., they are more likely to make the right choices.

It would appear from the above that we are doing most things right. Why then are not all of our 'past pupils' shining examples of success. Some are in prison, some are chronic drug addicts, many are unemployed. Surely if they had the benefit of the comprehensive service outlined in this paper, they would be equipped with the skills and the motivation to alter their non-productive, destructive lives?

My experience leads me to conclude that a major factor contributing to this situation is the fact that we get to work with these children when they have committed serious crimes, when they are approximately fifteen years of age, when they are out of control of their families, when they are distrustful of adults and when society has labelled them as failures. To use medical terminology 'it would appear that we are treating the symptoms while the disease remains unaffected'.

Targeting the Community

I firmly believe that we should be tackling the problem of juvenile offending where it begins - in the community. The early warning signs are there. Absentee parents, one of the parents and/or siblings in prison, drug dependency in the home situation, truancy from school, contact with the Juvenile Liaison Scheme. These children are known to the authorities, so why are we (the authorities) not doing something about it?

I believe that there are two fundamental reasons: first, the state agencies that the child and the family are in contact with are operating in isolation. I have become acutely aware of this for the following reason. I have recently become involved in a European funded initiative known as SITYA. 'Sharing Information on Troubled Young Adults'. Whilst the thrust of the project is information technology driven, it demands that the three Government Departments with responsibility for children, Health, Education and Justice, work together to share information on troubled young adults, not just in Ireland but amongst other European countries also.

As part of my work on this project I identified a case study where the three Departments failed to share information on one particular child. The effect of this failure to share information was expensive with many staff in various agencies making the same mistakes. The parents of the child lost confidence in the professionals because, as they had to repeat the answers to the same questions over and over again they felt that nobody was listening. Finally the child became lost in all of this as it appeared that every agency had a very good reason why they could not care for him/her instead of working together in the interest of that child. Eventually the child had to be sent to the USA to be cared for. This was a sad indictment of our 'care system'.

Secondly, this community-based approach to tackling juvenile delinquency is a long-term approach. It does not offer a 'quick fix' and therefore there are very few votes for politicians to gain from implementing such a long-term strategy. However the present Government has appointed a Minister of State at the Department of Health with responsibility for Children. This was a most welcome appointment. Whilst the Minister has made it clear that while he will increase the capacity of the Children Detention Centres to enable them to accept all referrals (which could be termed 'widening the net but thinning the mesh'), he has stated that he will fully support community-based initiatives designed to avoid youngsters getting involved in crime.

When planning community approaches to adequately address the question 'what works with juvenile delinquents' I would agree with the recommendations of David Farrington, Professor of

Psychological Criminology at the University of Cambridge, Professor Farrington cites a combination of the following strategies when commenting on Prevention Techniques:

- Frequent home visiting by health care professionals to women during pregnancy and support during the child's infancy.
- Pre-School intellectual enrichment programmes designed to stimulate thinking and reasoning ability amongst children.
- Parenting Education Programmes.
- Cognitive and Social Skills training for children.
- Peer influence strategies.
- Classroom management for teachers.
- Anti-bullying initiatives in schools.

In addition to the implementation of Professor Farrington's recommendations I would envisage a Community Centre building as a vital component. This building will become the focal point of the community and must be situated in the heart of the disadvantaged area. This Community Centre must have adequate facilities in terms of space and in terms of equipment. It must be capable of being used by young people (youth club). It must be capable of storing equipment e.g. gardening tools for helping the elderly to tend their gardens. It must have a crèche facility where mothers can leave their children, under supervision, while they attend parenting classes, educational classes or even attend 'coffee mornings' in an effort to build community spirit. This Community Centre must be provided with an adequate number of trained Youth and Community Workers who can help the community to help itself.

Once the community has regained its sense of identity then a sense of pride will ensue. It is this sense of pride that will sustain a community and will ensure that when its children are hovering on the edge of involvement in offending behaviour, the community will do all it can to turn that child away from a life of crime.

Conclusion

In these days of booming economies and intellectual advancement, I believe that the politicians can be persuaded, by the knowledge that abounds on the subject of juvenile delinquency, by the examples of communities that have succeeded and by the academics and the practitioners, that this problem can be successfully addressed.

References

Bailleau, F. (1996) 'Social Crime Prevention: Juvenile Delinquency' in Asquith S. (ed) *Children and Young People in Conflict with the Law,* London: Sage.

Bates, B. F. (1996) *Aspects of Childhood Deviancy: A Study of Young Offenders in Open Centres in the Republic of Ireland,* Unpublished Dissertation, University College Dublin.

Corrado, R., Bala, N., Linden, R., Le Blanc, M. (1992) *Juvenile Justice in Canada: A Theoretical and Analytical Assessment,* Vancouver: Butterworth.

Farrington, D. (1995) *Understanding and Preventing Youth Crime*: A Study for the Rowntree Foundation, York.

Government of Ireland (1996) *First report of The Select Committee on Crime, its Causes and Remedies,* Dublin: Government Publications.

Government of Ireland (1996) *The Children Bill 1996* (Juvenile Justice), Dublin: Government Publications.

Junger-Tas, J. (1994) 'Delinquent Behaviour Amongst People in the Western World': Ministry of Justice: Amsterdam in Bailleau, F.(ed*) Social Crime Prevention: Juvenile Delinquency.*

Lipsey, T. (1989*)* 'The Efficacy of Intervention for Juvenile Delinquency': Results from 400 Studies, Paper presented to the Annual Meeting (41st) of the American Society of Criminology, Reno, Nevada in Corrado et al. (1992) *Juvenile Justice in Canada,* Vancouver: Butterworth.

MacDonald, B. (1993) 'A Political Classification of Evaluation Studies' in *Social Research, Philosophy, Politics and Practice*, Hammersley, M. (ed), London: Sage.

Martinson, R. (1974) What Works? - Questions and Answers about Prison Reform, *The Public Interest*, 35, pp22-54.

Palmer T. (1992) *The Re-Emergence of Correctional Intervention*, London: Sage.

Pearson, G. (1983) *Hooligan : A History of Respectable Fears*, London: Macmillan.

Stewart, G. & Tutt, N. (1987) *Children in Custody*, Aldershot: Avebury.

Wall, A.C.B. (1997a) *The Children Bill, 1996: 'Children in custody – giving them their Just Desserts !'*, Unpublished Dissertation, The Queens University, Belfast.

Wall, A.C.B. (1997b) *The Milieu Practice of Care*: Paper presented to the British Criminology Conference at The Queens University, Belfast.

MULTI-AGENCY WORKING AND THE FAST TRACKING OF PERSISTENT YOUNG OFFENDERS

Phil Dinham, City and County of Cardiff, Wales

Introduction

This paper sets out to illustrate the benefits of multi-agency working in the context of the "Fast Tracking" initiative for persistent young offenders. In its election manifesto, the New Labour Government of 1997 pledged to halve the time between arrest and sentence, from an average of one hundred and forty two days to seventy-one. The Audit Commission, in its important review of the Youth Justice System in England and Wales, "Misspent Youth" (Audit Commission Publications 1996), documented the problems and waste caused by such delay, particularly the financial and resource costs to the Police and the Courts.

Local Historical Context

Like many Local Authority areas, Cardiff has received its share of media attention centred around the exploits of a few prolific juvenile offenders, the response to which had been a "blame culture" where Crown Prosecution Service, Social Services and Police very publicly went on record to attribute to each other the responsibility for a youth's growing list of offences committed on bail. Information and statistics were used to score points rather than understand the problem. Local Government reorganisation, with Cardiff emerging as a new Unitary Authority in April 1996, added operational difficulties to youth justice services when previously amalgamated specialist resources were disaggregated and had to re-form to deliver a parallel range of services within two new unitary authority areas. Cardiff, then, was not a promising place to begin a multi-agency "fast track" scheme.

The Imperatives to Fast Track

Both the Home Office and Lord Chancellor's Department have given the clearest guidance on their expectation that constituent agencies within the youth justice system will meet individual and joint performance targets and deliver the manifesto pledge. However, delay is not only wasteful of resources, it breaks the link in the mind of the young person between the crime and its repercussions. It exposes the young person to the increased risks of offending whilst on bail - and breaches of bail give Local Authorities and Prison Services the increased costs and concerns associated with confining a remanded young offender. Delays in dealing with offences often prevent essential services getting to the young person at a time when they are most likely to have a positive effect. Delay can also be distressing to the victim of crime and has brought the youth justice system into disrepute within the community it seeks to serve.

The fact that Cardiff was chosen by the Audit Commission as a pilot site for the "Misspent

Youth" research and the subsequent District Audit follow-up in 1997, meant that we had both a national and local perspective on the issue of delay. Two important groups - the "Magistrates' Court User Group" and the "Cardiff Juvenile & Young Offenders Co-ordinating Committee", both received distilled information which highlighted issues of delay at 3 key management points -

i	between arrest and decision to prosecute
ii	between decision to prosecute and first Court appearance
iii	between first Court appearance and eventual disposal

We also identified that although locally our "Not Guilty" pleas within the Youth Court ran at 70%, the national figure was only 43%. This was leading to a great many 'collapsed' trials after time had been set aside for contests.

What happened next was the critical factor. We had the information, we had the multi-agency forum for debating the information. We also had the Central Government imperative to resolve the problem. However, most important of all was a local commitment to work together - Crown Prosecution Service, Court Clerks, Police, Probation and Social Services, to help each other, to understand each other's difficulties and, most importantly, to find new solutions rather than old excuses.

The Cardiff Context

What works for Cardiff is not necessarily a solution that will work, unmodified, everywhere else where delay is an issue. Cardiff has a particular set of local characteristics which have shaped the fast-tracking model it has developed:

- it is a relatively small geographical area (approximately 12 miles x 6 miles)
- it has a condensed urban population of around 320,000
- 32,000 of the population are aged 10-18 years who commit around 2,800 recorded offences each year.
- there is one Youth Court area served from one Central Court, with 2-3 Courts sitting each weekday. In a year the Court processes around 1,000 offences.
- most Cardiff young offenders commit their crimes within the local area

The people responsible for operational management are a small group who have had the opportunity, through existing forums, to meet and establish relationships. There are just three police divisions while Social Services and Probation have close service delivery links through an agreed protocol and the Crown Prosecution Service have established a team of 3 specialist Youth Court prosecutors.

From within this group a small 'project team' was delegated the task of developing a fast-tracking model for Cardiff. The team comprised a Police Inspector, the Probation Manager responsible for Magistrates' Court work, the Crown Prosecution team leader for Youth Courts, the Clerk to the Youth Court and Youth Justice Manager. The small number involved aided positive debate and, importantly, the group had delegated authority to plan and implement the final model. What I found crucial to the practical and progressive working of the group was a common understanding, from the outset, regarding the objective of fast-tracking. We were clear about the effect of delay - on the community, on the victims of crime, on the resources and frustrations of those involved in the Youth Justice process and on the young person. We saw that by resolving delay we would bring appropriate, timely intervention (not just a fast-track to custody) to the young person. That intervention, if effective, benefits not just the young person but the victim and the wider community. We focused on "making the first Court appearance effective".

Working Together

There are three main levels to multi-agency working :

i	Strategic
ii	Operational Management
iii	Practice

The Project Group in Cardiff had received its strategic mandate from the Home Office and Lord Chancellor's Department and locally from the two key forums previously mentioned (the Court Users' Group and Juvenile & Young Offender Co-ordinating Committee). It also had the support of two further key local forums - firstly the Local Authority Community Safety Group, keen to develop its "Crime Prevention Strategy" in advance of the new statutory duty outlined in the Crime and Disorder Act. Secondly, the "Youth Justice Forum" for South Wales, comprising the Chief Police Officer, Chief Probation Officers and Directors of Social Services within the South Wales Police Force Area. Given the cross boundaries issues which had arisen between the seven new Unitary Authorities, relationships within this group, particularly around issues such as resources and costings arising out of comparative data provided by the District Auditor, were interesting to say the least. At a strategic level it has also been interesting to see fresh evidence of dialogue between different Government departments - Home Office and Department of Health, Home Office and Education, Home Office and Lord Chancellor - to ensure that separate policies pursued within individual departments (for example to reduce legal aid expenditure, to combat school exclusion, to combat youth drug and alcohol misuse) collectively contribute to youth crime reduction strategies. Given this lead from the centre, hopefully extending to all aspects of social policy including housing and employment, the message for local politicians regarding multi-agency solutions which extend across unitary boundaries is clear.

In terms of operational management, the project team worked from the previously mentioned common understanding of the positive reasons behind reducing delay. We were open to criticism of existing practices which contributed to delay and prepared to go back to our host agencies and say the same things there that we were saying within the project group. From a youth justice perspective, this meant opening negotiations about the role of the Cautioning Panel, sharing information with the Crown Prosecution Service at practitioner level regarding individual cases, discussing methods of reducing offending on bail, and more timely preparation of Pre Sentence Reports, within the "21 working day" National Standard.

The model that evolved centred around a process which would deliver a "Court outcome" within 71 days and which contained a number of key operational and time management standards which practitioners could agree as being achievable without compromising quality standards. These included -

i) **From Arrest to Decision to Prosecute**

- Clear definition of a 'persistent offender' eligible for fast-tracking, to enable Custody Sergeants to make on the spot decisions to charge and bail to Court date[1].

- Full file preparation commences at that point - no delay while cautioning decision debated.

ii) **From Decision to Prosecute to first Court Date**

Full file to Crown Prosecution within 3 weeks of offence.

- Young offender bailed to Court 5 weeks after offence (unless bail refused, when Court is fixed for next day).

- Police Custody Sergeants and Court Clerks given regular lists of 'persistent' offenders to enable first Court date to be tied into prosecutor handling those cases (the 3 specialist prosecutors each take ownership of the total 'persistent' offenders to facilitate an overview of proceedings).

- Advance disclosure to defence solicitors before first Court date.

- CPS examine any fresh offences against existing charges and determine (in consultation with police and having regard to victim issues) whether prosecution is essential.

- Presumption that legal aid will be granted in all youth cases.

iii) **From First Court Hearing to Sentence**

- Specialist Prosecutor aims to obtain plea at first hearing - Magistrates aim to allow defence time on the day to consult with young person regarding plea.

- CPS consider balance of guilty pleas versus not guilty pleas and determine how best to proceed with not guilty pleas.

- If 'not guilty', trial date set 4 weeks after first hearing.

---

[1] The Government's definition of a persistent offender is "someone aged 10-17 who has been sentenced for one or more recordable offences on three or more separate occasions and is arrested again within 3 years of last being sentenced.

- If guilty plea, 3 weeks allowed for Pre Sentence Report (if fresh offences occur during 3 week PSR adjournment, author will provide verbal/addendum information on the day of sentence to revise PSR and include fresh offences).

- Magistrates 'geared up' to question validity of any request for adjournment.

This gives a time scale of -

From arrest to first Court date	-	5 weeks (35 days)
From guilty plea to sentence	-	3 weeks (if PSR required) (21 days)
From first Court date to finding of guilt (or acquittal)	-	4 weeks (28 days)

Consequently,

From arrest to sentence without PSR	-	35 days
From arrest to sentence with PSR (Guilty plea)	-	56 days
From arrest to sentence with PSR (following conviction)	-	84 days

Outcomes and "Spin-Offs"

Thus far only a small number (around 40) young offenders have completed the fast-track process. Initial monitoring shows that all were in Court within 5 weeks of the arrest which triggered fast-tracking. Seventy per cent entered a guilty plea at that hearing. The others either entered a guilty plea or were convicted at the second hearing and the average number of days between arrest and sentence is thirty[2].

The longest period between arrest and sentence monitored was 64 days and the average number of Court appearances was two.

The sample number is small and the period covered is just the initial 3 months of the scheme (1 December 1997 to 1 March 1998) where enthusiasm was at its height. Longer term evaluation is needed to confirm whether the gains are sustainable. Some issues emerging revolve around cases of non-appearance where warrants are issued and a local issue concerning young people changing solicitors mid proceedings. We are finding less "Not Guilty" pleas, possibly due to the CPS/Defence dialogue before or at the initial hearing.

There is no evidence of discrimination in sentencing patterns of fast-track youths, though this is difficult to measure given the facts that the numbers monitored thus far are small and tend

---

[2] This figure is lower than the target of 35 days as it includes a number of remands into custody or Local Authority accommodation where the 5 week delay between arrest and first Court appearance is obviated.

to be at higher risk of custody due to the frequency and seriousness of their offending. Initial findings suggest a reduction in time spent on remand prior to sentencing.

Outside the focus of the fast-track objectives, the other gains have been extremely positive. Overall, there is a greater degree of dialogue and a willingness to help each other troubleshoot further problems - such as offending by young people in Local Authority accommodation, sharing of Pre Sentence Reports with CPS, liaison over remand and bail conditions. We have made it not just acceptable but commonplace for day to day practice concerns to be discussed and resolved within a framework of mutual benefit. We have also been able to contribute to the national development of fast-tracking and helped place issues such as legal aid decision making and the inclusion of defence solicitors in the process, on the national agenda. There is, perhaps, a developing sense of being part of a "youth justice system" with shared objectives.

Outstanding Issues

Above, I highlighted some of the concerns about longer-term evaluation to see if the current gains are sustainable. At present the Magistrates' Courts in England and Wales are under pressure to reduce delay overall, not just in youth work, and possibly the Cardiff Youth Court is seen as relatively resource-rich and pressure may be there to redistribute resources and Court time to the Magistrates' Court.

The five week pre-Court delay needs further examination to see whether an abbreviated file preparation process could reduce this to two weeks without adversely affecting the effectiveness of the first Court appearance.

Also, although the Home Office are clear that within the consistent national target for fast-tracking there is room for local solutions, South Wales Police are keen to establish Force-wide procedures across Court Area boundaries, Probation Area boundaries and the 7 Unitary Authority Areas. Consequently, the part local politics is to play has yet to unfold - not just in fast-tracking but in the overall delivery of the Crime and Disorder Act, particularly Part III and the formation of local Youth Offending Teams and Youth Offending Plans.

Ultimately, the test of multi-agency working in the field of youth offending is very simple. If it works for young people, that is if it delivers timely, effective intervention that prevents and reduces offending, then it also works for the benefit of victims of youth crime. If it works for young people, it works for the wider community where those young people today identified as offenders or potential offenders, become socially integrated. Consequently, fast-tracking is an important first step in making youth justice more relevant to the community, the victims of crime and the young offender.

A SCOTTISH CUSTODIAL PERSPECTIVE

Dan Gunn, Governor, HM Young Offenders' Institute, Polmont, Scotland

My aim is to offer an overview of the custody role, an analysis of the pressures for change and appraisal of our current agenda. There is now considerable interest in Scotland in the management of young offenders.

I have structured the paper into three sections. The first related to selected background issues followed by selected current issues. In conclusion I attempt to address specifically the issue of exclusion to inclusion all addressed from the perspective of working in a custodial environment.

A. Selected Background Issues

From Borstal to YOI

There was a consensus in the late 1960s and 1970s that Borstal was outmoded and had outlived its usefulness. This was partly due to the collapse of confidence in the rehabilitation model and the increasing concerns regarding the indeterminate sentence and the formidable discretionary power given to its staff and management. The primary argument for change however was to move the assessment of the convicted young offender from the Courts to the Prison Authorities. The old borstal report, which involved an assistant governor recommending one of up to seven available disposals, was replaced by a generic sentence allowing penal practitioners to decide where a young offender should be best placed. Sadly it is all too evident that over the past 15 years this model has not prospered north or south of the border. What has happened is that the YOI regime has evolved as being very similar to that of a Prison and arguably the difference between a YOI and a prison is purely one of nomenclature. It is this issue that is now somewhat belatedly being addressed as a matter of priority by both Prison Services.

Population trends

Unlike England, the population over a 5 year period in Scotland has been stable, although this does mask considerable variations year by year. On average we have between 700 and 800 convicted young offenders and between 200 and 300 on remand. The two key developments over the past 5 years is that the YOs have been given much longer sentences and there has been a marked increase in what one could term 'vulnerable' young offenders. These developments reflect a similar situation with adult offenders.

Opportunity and responsibility

This was the name of a SPS Policy document issued in 1990 with regard to the management of long-term prisoners (LTPs). This document was much acclaimed at the time and has given the SPS an aspirational and inspirational agenda for the 1990s which is still ongoing. Our new philosophy was based on a radical change in the mindset that LTPs should be regarded as essentially 'responsible' and the approach, therefore, should be to offer a menu of opportunities, supported by a training strategy designed to empower professional Prison officers to act in the role of facilitator. Although designed to help manage an increasingly diverse and demanding adult population, the SPS has increasingly used this model for all categories of offenders with varying degrees of success. My approach at Polmont over the last 2 years has been to put theory into practice and to take forward the concept of linking the opportunity and responsibility agenda to young offenders and the management of the YOI in a meaningful and effective way. One of the key features of the model is the term 'normalisation', by which we mean that a prison seeks to reflect the external environment inside as far as possible, thereby normalising the environment. This gives us an immediate problem in that for the past 30 years society has deemed an 18 year old as an adult. There are numerous anomalies in the application of adulthood as they are based on distinctions between the ages of 16, 17 and 18 and not between 18 and 21.

The first issue then for practitioners is to reflect on the wide age group with which YOIs are expected to deal with: 15-21 year olds in England and Wales and those aged 16-21 years in Scotland. In England, I believe, there is considerable separation between the under 18s and the rest of the YOI population, although this has not been the case in Scotland. However, in November 1997 at Polmont, we did start an experiment with turning over one of our best accommodation units to first offender under 18s with the expressed intention of trying to reduce the risk of re-offending. To date this initiative has been remarkably well received by young offenders, their families and staff within the Institution. It is, of course, early days but we believe we have made a promising beginning, offering a different institutional ethos in terms of the relationship between staff and the young offender and with greater emphasis on family contact.

The Link between Adolescence and Criminality

We know that many young men will engage in delinquent behaviour while young but will not go on to become serious adult criminals. Our belief is that custody has a role to play in preparing them to appreciate that actions have consequences. Part of adolescence, as we can all recall, is about trying to grow up quickly, seeking to be older than our chronological age and being at the very least suspicious of all forms of authority. This makes our young offender population extremely difficult to support and to help. Our intervention can all too easily be written off as interference. The involvement of the Prison Psychologist has helped to change the staff development strategy by concentrating on the need to understand adolescence as a first critical stage in helping staff manage young offenders in their care in an appropriate fashion.

Exclusion

We must recognise that by the time a young person has come to a YOI he has already been excluded from society in many key respects. The reality of coming to a YOI arguably is the most extreme, tangible and public form of exclusion possible. The YO has now reached the 'total institution' with all that this entails. Goffman's analysis half a century ago has still many lessons for us, despite all the progress we might think we have made. From the YO's perspective, he has reached the end of the road, the last resort available to sentencers and is now excluded from society, his family and friends. The task facing SPS is to prepare the YO for his eventual return to society 'from exclusion to inclusion' while recognising that the YO population in large part consider themselves excluded from a society perceived as adult i.e. disinterested and non-responsive.

B. Selected Current Issues

Public Confidence
While there is a fundamental desire on the part of all youth organisations to act as the advocate for the individual, nevertheless there is a wider dimension of public confidence to be addressed by the UK Prison Services which we neglect at our peril. Focusing on public confidence leads us to adopt a cautious approach. With regard to the sensitive area of home leave, we are developing a risk assessment model to bring a degree of rigour and consistency to what can be a highly subjective process. I do not think we should be negative or defensive about this but recognise that public protection is paramount and as public servants we should respect and address the concerns that do arise from time to time in our communities.

Institutional Culture

Total institutions do have a very strong culture which must be taken into account in any assessment of their performance and values. The YOI culture in Scotland seems to have developed as a rather static one with no internal pressure for change. Staff operate within an authoritarian paternalistic continuum with an entrenched emphasis on formality and distance. Young people have concerns and worries which are invariably with each other and occasionally with staff on an individual basis but they are not prepared individually or collectively to challenge the boundaries of policy. It will be interesting to see how long this relatively passive and compliant approach will last with the advent of the Children's Act and its pressure on all organisations to be seen to be consulting with young people. In my judgement, the current YOI culture has to change and to change quickly.

Normalisation

This is one of the key themes arising from our Opportunity and Responsibility Agenda mentioned above. By normalisation, I mean that what happens outside should happen inside unless there are specific reasons relating to security where such change would not follow. The time lag that used to exist between what happened in a Prison and what happened in the Community has reduced dramatically and is continuing to reduce. The values and attitudes of external society are now being rapidly replicated internally with the collapse of deference and automatic respect for authority. Key areas of change for us are the now widespread use of first names at all levels within the organisation, the need to evolve a robust, transparent and responsive complaints system and in general to adopt an even more open policy towards the media and to local communities where prisons are located.

Age Span

In England and Wales the age span is 15-21 years with a divide at 17 years, in Scotland we operate on a basis of 16-21years. The first attempt in Scotland to look at the needs of the under 18 population was made by the organisation, Scottish Association for the Study of Delinquency (SASD) in 1993 and their report's conclusions helped to influence my thinking. There are, however, various age groupings that deserve critical attention including under 18s, 18-21 year olds, 18-25 year olds. In terms of normalisation, arguably we should be abolishing Young Offenders Institutions and treating all individuals sentenced to prison at the age of 18 and above as adults. This view has its advocates and I am in part persuaded by this approach. The question is how do we balance age with maturity and other variables. The debate undoubtedly will and should go on but meanwhile at Polmont we have started an under 18 unit which we will monitor carefully and possibly expand to separate all under 18s from the rest of the establishment in due course.

Knowledge Base

Here the issue is the lack of an up-to-date knowledge base. This is particularly true in Scotland and research has been commissioned which will be published in late 1998, which will give us an up-to-date profile of the young offender population, their background, their lifestyle and hopefully some insights into their levels and degrees of criminality.

Partnership

There are two elements to consider here: the first, is related to the community and for the need for YOIs to work much more closely with the non-custodial disposals available to the Courts and to the Children's Hearing System. In time perhaps, as part of a pre-release course, young offenders could attend appropriate community based disposals. Polmont has had the first young offender involved in The Prince's Trust Volunteers and re-established its involvement with The Duke of Edinburgh Scheme. There are numerous other opportunities available to Young Offenders Institutions.

The other level of partnership is within the Criminal Justice System and the need for all the other Criminal Justice agencies to work together. At present the Criminal Justice System is much more of a process, arguably more inconsistent than consistent and unstructured rather than structured. There is tremendous scope here for effective partnership with the advent of the Scottish Parliament controlling a fully devolved Criminal Justice System. The opportunities for a meaningful change in policies and working practices are undoubtedly there and it is up to the professionals involved to ensure the new processes on offer work to the satisfaction of society.

Staff

I would like to highlight three issues here – selection, training and role.

In the past, selection has not been specifically for Young Offenders Institutions. This arguably has been a mistake but has recently been corrected. However, it will take time for the new selection process to bear fruit.

In terms of training, there is a need to address the peculiar needs of our population irrespective of the debates surrounding normalisation. The Trust for the Study of Adolescence has pioneered a course, The Nature of Adolescence, which was warmly endorsed by Sir David Ramsbottom in his Thematic Review and is now pursued as a matter or priority in Polmont. In the long-term establishments, as part of delivering the opportunity and Responsibility agenda, the facilitator role is reasonably well established with sentence planning, now re-launched sentence management, as the catalyst for change. A new model is needed for a YOI where increasingly staff spend less time doing things to YOs and more time doing things with them. The role of an officer in a YOI is becoming even more challenging, complex and above all multi-dimensional.

Addressing Offending Behaviour

This is, in part, a continuation of my last point about the new role for staff. In Scotland, staff are being trained to deliver programmes, more and more of which are becoming accredited and subject to rigorous monitoring. Polmont's priorities are to develop cognitive skills and anger management programmes but there is a huge range of courses that need to be developed and delivered relating to drugs, alcohol, health education, health promotion, sex offending, etc. The adult strategy is based on individual need but consideration is being given to offering a different model for young offenders by making certain assumptions, as to what courses are required and thereby not taking up valuable limited time simply on assessment. This model is in its infancy but is being developed as a matter of urgency.

Mental Health

I have become very conscious of this issue in the literature which has emanated from England. Recently, Peter Wilson, Director of Young Minds, defined mental health as a series of incapacities and that young people are more and more suffering from a lack of various capacities, such as a lack of emotional well-being. In Scotland, the definition of Mental Health has been very narrow tending to focus on diagnosis of mental illness and treatment. As we develop the training of Prison Officers, it is hoped that they will play a key role in developing the capacities of our young people. Undoubtedly the debate will be revisited with renewed vigour and rigour.

Family

In the early 1990s, as a result of the first ever Climate Survey, enhanced family contact became a critical objective for SPS and has improved facilities for visits, visitors and formed links with relevant organisations to assist in meeting the needs of everyone involved. Family Contact Development officers have been introduced and found to be highly beneficial. Unfortunately this approach has had a limited impact on YOIs. The relationship between young offenders and their families seems to be even more complicated and frequently traumatic than that of adults. Young people are at a critical stage of moving from one family to another from the old to the new, neither of which is at all stable. There is also a group of young men who seem to be attracted to older women who often have children by previous relationships which are slowly being acknowledged. Only by working together can the relevant agencies offer meaningful support.

C. From Exclusion to Inclusion

This is the theme of the Conference. My task within the custodial setting is to deliver the Mission Statement which has 4 components: Security, Order, Care and Opportunity. My vision is that we will seek to intervene effectively to change a young person who is marginalised and increasingly alienated from, arguably, an intolerant and unresponsive society into a young man with a future, with a sense of citizenship and a perceived recognition that he has a stake in his society. The custodial experience need not be about purely punishment and retribution. Prison can and does represent a real chance to change.

With regard to the individual, our first priority is to address his needs with regard to his offending and thereby reduce the risk to society, to his family and to himself. An initial priority is the issue of identity. We notice in a national institution, such as Polmont, that when young people are excluded from society they re-form their social groupings to avoid reforming their identity. They take comfort in 'tribal' activity which is a convenient alternative to addressing their own personal situation. A problem for young people in and out of custody is their personal safety. Many young people are victims as well as perpetrators and they need to develop skills in relation to conflict resolution and assertiveness. Finding practical ways of keeping themselves safe in their own communities without redress to a cycle of violence, weapons and retaliation is a complex challenge.

Overall, there is a need to develop individual consciousness, notably of their value as a person and their value to their 'family' and their 'community'. In terms of their offending, they can begin to be made aware of the consequence of their actions through inputs from Victim Support. Their understanding of society and what society has to offer can be expanded through schemes such as those mentioned earlier: The Duke of Edinburgh Award Scheme and The Prince's Trust Volunteers.

Internally, a strategy based on risk reduction will extend to addressing the more tangible areas – education, employability and employment itself. While there is a focus on critical self-assessment of the culture and developing initiatives addressing psychological and concrete areas of need, the approach is also to look outward to what society can, should and hopefully will offer over time.

The question is: what is society prepared to do to help its young people in trouble? American child development literature has coined the emotive phrase 'toxic environment' which I think captures many of the problems and concerns associated with home in the minds of our young offenders. Prison can be viewed as a relatively safe and predictable haven where a young person knows his place and can work within the structures that exist there. The environment outside however, is hostile, unpredictable, threatening and fundamentally unwelcoming. The new government is openly stating that it is committed to addressing the conditions which induce criminal behaviour. There are many support mechanisms in place but do they all project themselves appropriately and engage effectively with young offenders in need? There again is a need for team work as well as visibility. Material resources are important but the use of human resources is even more important and the way to make the most of all our resources is surely to enhance integration and inclusion of all various agencies. Society needs to be persuaded, encouraged and even cajoled into reaching out its difficult and troubled young people. If our various criminal justice agencies can convince the public to have confidence in the way we are doing and in particular in addressing crime effectively, them our communities may well become more tolerant. With measured, targeted and appropriate intervention supported by team work at all levels, I believe we can reduce exclusion and in time deliver inclusion.

The task is immense but we can and should be optimistic. Home Affairs Minister Henry McLeish has defined the task as:

> *'Young people need to feel that society has a place for them and that they have a stake in society. This is a question of self-esteem, self confidence, self respect and a question of aspiration. Young people need to have a vision of what they can achieve'.*

We all know that where there is no vision people perish. It is in everyone's interest that our young people in trouble do not perish.

SUMMARY OF KEY CONCLUSIONS FROM PLENARY SESSIONS

Gill Stewart, The Scottish Office

National Group Discussions

Delegates were given the opportunity to break into National Groupings to discuss the issues raised by the various speakers in the previous six plenary sessions. Each group, thereafter, reported back to the full conference, highlighting those issues and problems which, for them, had been distinctive features of the conference.

Wales

- National frameworks were important and provided a distinctive focus for a conference such as this but the Urban/Rural distinction was also very powerful and could represent equally distinctive cultural differences.

- One of the values of a conference such as this was the opportunity for information sharing with similar cultural and demographic areas in other jurisdictions.

- In a context of local authority re-organisation and pressure on resources, it had to be accepted that young offenders were not vote winners.

- In work with young offenders, continuity of treatment and through care was essential.

- We should never write off young offenders and a safety net should always be provided.

- We should always ask the question: What can the young offender offer the community?

Ireland

A number of important themes and issues had emerged from the conference.

- Full and accurate auditing was an essential pre-requisite of work within communities to prevent and tackle offending.

- Restorative justice was an increasingly important concept and body of practice.

- In developing a coherent national strategy for youth justice, it was valuable to look at examples from other jurisdictions. Representatives from particular jurisdictions had not necessarily all met together before as a single body.

- It was valuable to note that there were more points of commonality than there were differences between the five jurisdictions.

- More effort should be put into writing up the work and achievements of particular intervention programmes. It was important to disseminate valuable lessons.

- The conference had been very valuable and could be usefully repeated. Presentations had been of a high quality but future conferences should look for greater participation by delegates.

Northern Ireland

The conference had revealed a high commonality of aims but different methods for their achievement.

- The conference had highlighted the importance of interagency and community links.

- Regular evaluations of what works with young offenders were essential.

- Restorative justice was a useful and genuine option and efforts should be made to train those within education systems.

- As well as early intervention, timely intervention was also crucial.

- There was a need to encourage greater involvement from the education system.

- The conference had highlighted the importance of the alignment of policies across different government departments.

- The conference had also identified opportunities to make this happen without the necessity for legislation.

- In the context of Northern Ireland, there was a need for greater involvement from social services.

- Criminal justice systems needed to devise systems for regular monitoring. For example, the judicial system only saw offenders in 'short bites'.

- Offending was often only one aspect of a wider set of problem issues, often related to chosen lifestyles.

- Custody did not necessarily have to be a 'total waste of time'.

- The conference had been very useful and those from individual jurisdictions might wish to consider holding intermediate conferences within their own domestic settings. There was clearly a need within individual jurisdictions for more discussion.

England

- Restorative justice was important but not simply as a 'bolt-on'.

- Formal intervention in the lives of young offenders is not always the best option.

- There is a tendency towards parochialism within individual jurisdictions and a consequent failure to share practice. Conferences such as this one provide valuable opportunities to break out of that mould.

- Further conferences of this kind would be valuable but should aim to achieve greater discussion from delegates and greater use of specific case studies.

- In the context of England and Wales, it was believed that Youth Offending Teams would break trough the problems of achieving multi-agency partnerships.

Scotland

- There was a need for an integrated approach across the full range of agencies and services, including prisons.

- Restorative justice was a key element in the aim to achieve social inclusion and should not simply be seen as a 'bolt on' to the criminal justice system.

- There was a need for a fundamental review of funding and resourcing within the criminal justice system.

- Young offenders were first and foremost young people with potential and we should not abandon them.

- It was important to work in and with local communities.

- The Scottish Parliament would inevitably take time to establish itself and to rise to the challenges.

In Summary

Summarising the points which had arisen from the national groupings, Gill Stewart, Head of the then Scottish Office Social Work Services Group emphasised the value of mutual learning, both within and between jurisdictions. It was clear that we all had a common purpose. But how do we achieve those aims and objectives? The conference had identified the value of integration of services and the establishment of collaborative structures. The question remained about how well this could be achieved with and without legislation. At the end of the day, it was the people who worked within and for the system who mattered and who could make things happen. To harness those abilities and enthusiasm, however, there was a need for better structures at the local level.

Early intervention had been a key theme through out the conference but early intervention needed to be put in place as early as possible, at the most minimal level to be effective and it needed to be timely intervention.

The principles and practice of restorative justice had been enthusiastically grasped by the conference delegates and the view came through clearly that it must be fully integrated in to the criminal justice system. There was a belief that it provided a common sense way of dealing with problems.

Delegates from each of the five jurisdictions had given a strong vote of confidence to the conference and endorsed the view that similar conferences should be organised to bring together the five jurisdictions.

ANNEX A: Children in the Justice Systems in Britain and Ireland

By way of preparation for the Conference each of the jurisdictions was asked to provide a summary of their respective juvenile justice systems. The Scottish Office commissioned Ian Clark to prepare a paper on the juvenile justice system in Scotland and commissioned Olwyn Burke to summarise the legal position for the Republic of Ireland. Dr. Paul O'Mahony also provided a paper outlining the juvenile justice system in the Republic of Ireland based on detailed research and statistical evidence. For the position of Northern Ireland, delegates were referred to a Northern Ireland publication *A Beginner's Guide to Criminal Justice in Northern Ireland*, November 1997. As for England and Wales, delegates were provided with three different briefing papers from NACRO: *The Crime and Disorder Bill, The Crime and Disorder Bill – Implementation Guidance, A Brief Outline of the Youth Justice System in England and Wales.*

CHILDREN, YOUNG PEOPLE AND CRIME IN SCOTLAND

Ian Clark, Research Consultant

This paper describes the procedures which exist for dealing with children and young persons who are accused of crimes in Scotland. The description will be interspersed with statistics, showing the number of children referred to Reporters, referred to Children's Hearings and the number of children and young persons proceeded against in court, and the outcome of court proceedings.

To begin with, some contextual information. The number of live births has been declining for a number of years, dropping from 65,000 in 1983 to 60,000 in 1995. The 1991 Census figures show that there were 324,159 children aged between ten and fourteen, 312,288 aged between fifteen and nineteen, and 72,734 aged twenty. The proportion of births outside marriage has nearly trebled from 11.3% in 1980 to 33.8% in 1995 and the proportion of children under sixteen in families dependent on income support has risen to just over 25% in 1994. By the summer of 1994, 16,900 sixteen and seventeen year olds were estimated to be unemployed, even though the staying on rate has doubled from 21% of pupils continuing in publicly-funded secondary school education until sixth year in 1985-86 to 42% in 1996-97. The percentage who left at the minimum school leaving age fell from 46% in 1985-86 to 30% in 1995-96. The 1994 School Leavers Survey found that 60% of pupils truanted in their fourth year; 10% were persistent truants who had stayed away for days or weeks at a time.

A "child" is defined by section 97(2)(b) of the Children (Scotland) Act 1995 as a person under the age of sixteen years, someone over sixteen but under eighteen in respect of whom a supervision requirement is in force, or someone whose case has been referred to a Children's Hearing. The term also applies to truants over sixteen who are supposed to be still attending school. Section 41 of the Criminal Procedure (Scotland) Act 1995 reaffirmed earlier statute law by stating that "no child under the age of eight years can be guilty of any offence"; the age limit having been raised from seven to eight in 1932.

Until 1971, juvenile offenders (young persons aged under seventeen) were brought before Sheriff or Burgh Courts, apart from in the counties of Ayr, Fife and Renfrew, and in the city of Aberdeen, where special Juvenile Courts presided over by Justices of the Peace were empowered to take over this function in the 1930s. Even so, it was considered that children ought to be treated differently from adults, with the emphasis on education and reform rather than punishment.

In 1961, a Committee on Children and Young Persons was appointed "to consider the provisions of the law of Scotland relating to the treatment of juvenile delinquents and juveniles in need of care or protection or beyond parental control." It was chaired by Lord Kilbrandon, and a report of its findings was published in 1964. The report advocated separating the process of adjudication over contested allegations made against children from the process of considering what remedial measures ought to be taken in respect of both children who had admitted wrongdoing and children in need of care and protection. The paramount principle of the Kilbrandon Report was the recognition of the needs of the child as being the overriding consideration.

As a consequence, the Report proposed that young offenders under sixteen years of age should be referred to a Children's Hearing - a tribunal which is empowered to take decisions about the needs of children who are referred to it, and which comprises a sitting of three lay members (including at least one male and at least one female) of a Children's Panel. Panel members were expected to be volunteers from a wide range of backgrounds who had experience of and an interest in children's welfare and the ability to communicate well with children and their families.

Most of the Kilbrandon recommendations were accepted by the then Government, and the Social Work (Scotland) Act 1968 established the machinery for Children's Panels and Hearings, which came into effect in April 1971. Each regional and islands council appointed an official called the Reporter to the Children's Panel, whose main duties involved receiving reports on children from the police or other statutory or voluntary agencies, investigating the evidence in any such reports, deciding whether to refer the children in turn to a Children's Hearing and, in the event of the latter, providing appropriate legal advice to the Hearing. The Reporter may decide that a formal Hearing is unnecessary, but personally warn a child as to his future behaviour, or refer the child to the relevant Social Work Department and request that informal advice, guidance and assistance is provided for him.

Since 1971 few fundamental changes have been made to the Children's Hearing system. The Local Government etc. (Scotland) Act 1994 removed Reporters from the aegis of what would have been a larger number of smaller councils following local government reorganisation, and set up on a national basis the Scottish Children's Reporter Administration, under the control of a Principal Reporter, to take over the functions of the former regional Reporters. The Children (Scotland) Act 1995 gave Children's Hearings powers to make new orders in relation to children requiring specific types of supervision or protection.

The grounds for referral of a child to a Hearing are where a child:

- is beyond the control of his parents or guardian
- is falling into bad associations or is exposed to moral danger
- is likely to suffer unnecessarily or be seriously impaired in health or development due to a lack of parental care
- is a victim of an offence
- is, or is likely to become, a member of the same household as a child who is a victim of an offence
- is, or is likely to become, a member of the same household as a person who has committed offences against children
- is, or is likely to become, a member of the same household as a victim of sexual offences (incest or unlawful intercourse with a child) committed by a member of that household
- has failed to attend school regularly without reasonable excuse
- has committed an offence
- has misused alcohol or any drug
- has misused a volatile substance by deliberately inhaling its vapour
- is being provided with accommodation by a local authority or is the subject of a parental responsibilities order and his behaviour is such that special measures are necessary for his adequate supervision in his interest or in the interests of others

Throughout Scotland in 1995 there were 27,606 referrals to Reporters on alleged offence grounds. A total of 41,901 alleged offences were referred; an increase of 6% on 1994. Referrals on alleged offence grounds constituted 69% of all referrals of boys (22,826 referrals) and 32% of all referrals of girls (4,780 referrals). Of the referrals made on alleged offence grounds, 89% were made by local police and 8% were made by the Procurator Fiscal. Referrals on alleged truancy grounds constituted 7% of all referrals of boys (2,415 referrals) and 12% of all referrals of girls (1,821 referrals). Of the referrals made on alleged truancy grounds, 92% came from educational sources, 3% from local police, 2% from social work departments and 2% from parents.

Table 1
Number of offences per child by age group, 1995

Age at first referral in year		Number of offences per child, all referrals								Total offences referred	Average number of offences per child
		1	2	3	4-6	7-9	10-20	21+	Total children		
8-11	No.	1,219	280	133	114	45	39	7	1,837	3,880	2.11
	%	66	15	7	6	2	2	0	100		
12	No.	925	242	130	143	49	50	21	1,560	4,223	2.71
	%	59	16	8	9	3	3	1	100		
13	No.	1,489	474	238	296	116	109	41	2,763	8,227	2.98
	%	54	17	9	11	4	4	1	100		
14	No.	1,999	692	369	469	159	180	75	3,943	12,681	3.22
	%	51	18	9	12	4	5	2	100		
15	No.	2,427	770	412	442	159	184	31	4,425	11,944	2.70
	%	55	17	9	10	4	4	1	100		
16-17	No.	139	72	28	49	20	11	2	321	946	2.95
	%	43	22	9	15	6	3	0.6	100		
All ages	No.	8,198	2,530	1,310	1,513	548	573	177	14,849	41,901	2.82
	%	55	17	9	10	4	4	1	100		

Source: Scottish Office Statistical Bulletin "Referrals of Children to Reporters and Children's Hearings 1995-96", SWK/CH/1997/20, Table 6, May 1997.

Table 2
Initial action taken by Reporters on (selected) grounds referred, 1995 (%)

	Ground for referral	
Initial action by Reporter	Non-attendance at school	Offence
No action (total)	*33*	*61*
Under current supervision	*8*	*19*
Action on other grounds	*2*	*1*
Insufficient evidence	*1*	*4*
Compulsory care unnecessary	*22*	*36*
Referred to -		
Social work department	*17*	*6*
Police/juvenile liaison officer	*0*	*3*
Hearing	*50*	*30*
N (=100%)	4,236	27,606

Note: If more than one reason for referral is reported in a particular referral (or more than one offence alleged in an offence referral), it is described here as a "no action" case only if there is no action taken in respect of all the reasons (or offences) referred. Source: Scottish Office Statistical Bulletin "Referrals of Children to Reporters and Children's Hearings 1995-96", SWK/CH/1997/20, Table 7, May 1997.

Table 3
Children referred to a Reporter and a Hearing on offence grounds, by age and sex, 1995

Age at first referral in year	Number of offence referrals to Reporter		Number of offence referrals to Hearing	
	Boys	Girls	Boys	Girls
8-11	1,611	241	298	38
12	1,244	315	303	51
13	2,103	660	535	153
14	2,973	969	823	234
15	3,431	993	743	211
Total under 16	11,362	3,178	2,702	687

Source: Scottish Office Statistical Bulletin "Referrals of Children to Reporters and Children's Hearings 1995-96", SWK/CH/1997/20, Tables 8 and 9, May 1997.

A Children's Hearing begins by determining that the child is aged under sixteen. The grounds for referral are then explained, normally by the Chairperson. If the grounds are not accepted by the child or his parents or guardian, either the case may be referred to a Sheriff for adjudication within 28 days, or the referral to the Hearing will be discharged. If there is partial acceptance of the grounds, the Hearing may proceed. Hearings are conducted in private and, while bona fide representatives of the press may attend, they may not publish any details of the proceedings which could identify the child, or his or her address or school.

Table 4
Decision on grounds referred to a Hearing, 1995 (%)

| Type of ground | Total grounds referred to a Hearing (=100%) | Grounds not accepted and discharged by Hearing | Applications to a Sheriff on grounds | | | | Grounds accepted or established | |
			Abandoned by Reporter	Not established and discharged by Sheriff	Established	Total	Discharged by Hearing	Considered in disposal
Truancy	2,117	4	1	-	8	10	17	77
Offence	14,108	18	6	1	5	12	12	63

Note: Grounds/offences established are also included in either the "discharged by hearing" or "considered in disposal" columns. Offence figures relate to individual offences referred to a Hearing. Source: Scottish Office Statistical Bulletin "Referrals of Children to Reporters and Children's Hearings 1995-96", SWK/CH/1997/20, Table 11, May 1997.

If the grounds of referral are accepted or have been validated by a Sheriff and referred back, the Hearing will consider these grounds, any police or local authority reports and any other relevant information available to them. The case may be continued to a future Hearing for further information or discharged if supervision is considered unnecessary. Otherwise, the Hearing is likely to make a supervision requirement in respect of the child, which may specify where he is to reside and impose conditions limiting his association with specified persons, requiring him to undergo medical examination or treatment, requiring the location of the place of residence to be kept confidential, or requiring that a review Hearing be held within a specified time.

Table 5
Disposals by Hearings by sex, 1995

Disposals	Boys referred for offences only (1)		Boys referred for both offence and non-offence grounds (2)		Girls referred for offences only (3)		Girls referred for both offence and non-offence grounds (4)	
	No.	%	No.	%	No.	%	No.	%
Children not under supervision								
Case discharged	514	43	92	19	96	43	29	15
SR made	675	56	396	81	127	57	160	85
Other	10	1	2	-	1	-	0	0
Total	1,199	100	490	100	224	100	189	100
Children already under supervision								
Fresh grounds not considered:								
SR continued without variation	84	5	11	6	18	6	3	3
SR varied	54	3	16	8	18	6	17	20
SR terminated	139	9	6	3	18	6	4	5
Case discharged	168	11	5	3	13	4	4	5
SR continued without variation	548	34	69	35	102	33	21	24
SR varied	494	31	84	42	121	39	34	40
SR terminated	102	6	5	3	19	6	1	1
Other	7	-	2	1	1	-	2	2
Total	1,596	100	198	100	310	100	86	100
Total disposals	2,795		688		534		275	

Note: "SR" is a contraction of "Supervision requirement". Columns (2) and (4) include 37 and 27 transfer cases respectively. "Other" disposals includes transfer disposals and cases where no order was made by the Hearing. "Children already under supervision" includes outcomes of "precipitated" reviews where held. "Fresh grounds not considered" relates to cases where a child already under supervision was referred by the Reporter to a Hearing on fresh non-offence grounds or for fresh offences, but where these grounds (or offences) were subsequently not established by the Sheriff, abandoned by the Reporter or discharged by the Hearing. In such cases the disposal shown relates solely to the review of the existing SR only. "SR varied" includes disposals where the existing SR was terminated and a new one made. Source: Scottish Office Statistical Bulletin "Referrals of Children to Reporters and Children's Hearings 1995-96", SWK/CH/1997/20, Tables 12A(i) and 12A(ii), May 1997.

Table 6

Disposals by Hearings; details of Supervision Requirements if made or varied, 1995

Type of Supervision Requirement (SR)	Children referred for offences only		Children referred for both offence and non-offence grounds	
	No.	%	No.	%
Non-residential SR:				
Parent/Guardian	916	62	523	74
Relative/Friend	25	2	13	2
Foster parent	55	4	16	2
Other	23	2	4	1
Total	1,019	68	556	79
Residential SR:				
Local authority home	161	11	67	9
Voluntary home	8	1	0	0
Residential school	225	15	52	7
Other	76	5	32	5
Total	470	32	151	21
Total SRs made or varied	1,489	100	707	100

Note: This table is on the same basis as Table 5 above; figures in the "Total SRs made or varied" row correspond to the sum of the "SR made" and both the "SR varied" rows from Table 5, covering either new SRs which were imposed or existing ones which were varied. "Other non-residential" includes hospitals, special schools and other types of non-residential requirement. "Other residential" includes hostels, residential assessment centres and other types of residential requirement. Source: Scottish Office Statistical Bulletin "Referrals of Children to Reporters and Children's Hearings 1995-96", SWK/CH/1997/20, Table 12B, May 1997.

Table 7
Children under a current Supervision Requirement by type of supervision for selected grounds of original referral, 1995 (%)

Grounds of original referral	Type of SR	1995
Truancy	Parent/Guardian	*81*
	Relative/Friend	*3*
	Foster parent	*3*
	Other non-residential	*1*
	Local authority/voluntary home	*4*
	Residential school	*7*
	Other residential	*2*
	Total (=100%)	2,176
Offence	Parent/Guardian	*68*
	Relative/Friend	*2*
	Foster parent	*3*
	Other non-residential	*2*
	Local authority/voluntary home	*9*
	Residential school	*14*
	Other residential	*3*
	Total (=100%)	2,926

Note: Children originally referred on both the grounds listed will appear more than once in the Table. "Other non-residential" includes hospitals, special schools and other types of non-residential requirement. "Other residential" includes hostels, residential assessment centres and other types of residential requirement.   Source: Scottish Office Statistical Bulletin "Referrals of Children to Reporters and Children's Hearings 1995-96", SWK/CH/1997/20, Table 15C, May 1997

"Safeguarders" are appointed to protect the interests of the child where there is a conflict of interest between the child and the parents or guardian. During 1995, safeguarders were appointed in 38 cases (1%) out of the 3,329 disposals of children referred to Hearings exclusively on alleged offence grounds. Safeguarders were appointed in a further 27 cases (3%) out of the 963 disposals of children referred to Hearings on both offence and non-offence grounds.

After being notified that a Children's Hearing in respect of their case is to be held, children have the right to attend at all stages of the Hearing and are obliged to attend each stage unless their attendance is deemed unnecessary or if it is considered that it would be detrimental to their interests to attend. The Principal Reporter may ask the Hearing to issue a warrant to find the child, keep him or her in a place of safety until the Hearing and bring him or her before it. A warrant may also be issued if a child, having been notified about the Hearing, fails to attend.

Children may only be detained in a place of safety under a warrant for up to seven days before a Hearing; normally the Hearing will be convened before then, and the Principal Reporter will try to convene a Hearing on the first working day after the child is found. If a child has been arrested and detained in a place of safety, but no criminal charges are to be brought, the Principal Reporter is obliged to refer the child to a Children's Hearing. However, if the Principal Reporter considers that compulsory measures of supervision are not required, he can authorise the child's release from the place of safety.

The Hearing may grant a warrant to ensure the child attends or, if it considers it is necessary, that the child should be kept in a place of safety in order to safeguard or promote his welfare; initially for up to 22 days. The warrant may require the child to submit to medical or other examination and regulate his contact with any specified person or class of persons. Such a warrant may be continued in force for up to two additional 22-day periods. Thereafter, the Principal Reporter must apply to a Sheriff to keep the child in a place of safety for longer.

Table 8
Warrants and detentions, 1995

Detention/Warrant	Total 1995	%	Boys 1995	%	Girls 1995	%
Pre-hearing detentions:						
Offence	179	*18*	143	*26*	36	*8*
Place of safety	812	*82*	401	*74*	411	*92*
Total	991	*100*	544	*100*	447	*100*
Warrants:						
Continuation of pre-hearing detention	770	*46*	405	*44*	365	*48*
Continuation of Hearing	673	*40*	371	*40*	302	*39*
Child failing to attend Hearing	242	*14*	143	*16*	99	*13*
Child failing to attend application to Sheriff	2	*-*	2	*-*	0	*0*
Total	1,687	*100*	921	*100*	766	*100*

Source: Scottish Office Statistical Bulletin "Referrals of Children to Reporters and Children's Hearings 1995-96", SWK/CH/1997/20, Table 16, May 1997.

Table 9
Secure accommodation authorisations by age and sex, 1995

	Age group	SAA made	SAA continued
Boys	0-7	0	0
	8-11	2	3
	12	3	4
	13	10	14
	14	38	24
	15	37	72
	16-17	1	4
	All ages	91	121
Girls	0-7	0	0
	8-11	0	0
	12	2	0
	13	9	12
	14	19	20
	15	23	26
	16-17	3	4
	All ages	56	62
All children	Total	147	183

Note: "SAA" is a contraction of "Secure accommodation authorisations". Source: Scottish Office Statistical Bulletin "Referrals of Children to Reporters and Children's Hearings 1995-96", SWK/CH/1997/20, Table 17, May 1997.

An appeal may be lodged with a Sheriff within three weeks of a decision being made by a Children's Hearing. It will subsequently be heard by the Sheriff. If the appeal fails, the Sheriff confirms the decision of the Children's Hearing. If the appeal is allowed, any warrant to find and keep the child is recalled, and any supervision requirement imposed by the Hearing will cease to have effect. The Sheriff may remit the case back to the Children's Hearing for further consideration, discharge the child from being obliged to attend further Hearings in respect of the grounds for which the original Hearing was convened, or make a supervision requirement on whatever terms and conditions he considers appropriate. There were 145 appeals to a Sheriff against a Hearing's disposal in 1995. Of these, 100 failed and the Hearing's disposal was confirmed, six were upheld and the child discharged, while 39 were upheld and the case was remitted back to the hearing for further consideration.

Turning now to young persons and children involved with the criminal courts, Scottish Office statistics show the number of persons aged under twenty-one in respect of whom at least one charge was proved in Scotland during 1996. These data are disaggregated by age and main crime or offence in Table 10:

Table 10
Persons aged under 21 with a charge proved by main crime or offence in Scotland, 1996.

Main crime/offence	<16	16	17	Age 18	19	20	Total
All crimes & offences	160	2,857	7,201	8,802	8,024	8,122	35,166
All crimes	129	1,831	4,214	4,291	3,567	3,546	17,578
Non-sexual crimes of violence	32	177	410	385	302	320	1,626
Homicide	3	5	5	8	8	6	35
Serious assault	12	25	62	77	76	62	314
Handling offensive weapons	3	91	247	218	148	181	888
Robbery	13	54	94	74	62	68	365
Other	1	2	2	8	8	3	24
Crimes of indecency	7	10	31	24	30	41	143
Sexual assault	4	2	10	4	3	4	27
Lewd and libidinous practices	0	4	10	5	5	6	30
Other	3	4	11	15	22	31	86
Crimes of dishonesty	61	1,173	2,499	2,516	1,844	1,832	9,965
Housebreaking	5	236	472	448	327	348	1,836
Theft by opening lockfast places	5	173	347	368	261	231	1,385
Theft of motor vehicle	40	289	448	369	257	182	1,585
Shoplifting	2	134	423	490	339	372	1,760
Other theft	8	229	543	530	410	384	2,104
Fraud	0	10	40	62	83	113	308
Other	1	102	226	249	207	202	987
Fire-raising, vandalism etc.	13	267	494	472	415	370	2,031
Fire-raising	7	11	12	16	3	10	59
Vandalism, etc.	6	256	482	456	412	360	1,972
Other crimes	16	204	780	894	936	983	3,813
Crimes against public justice	15	127	548	562	554	502	2,308
Drugs	1	76	232	330	381	480	1,500
Other	0	1	-	2	1	1	5
All offences	31	1,026	2,987	4,511	4,457	4,576	17,588
Miscellaneous offences	16	786	2,103	2,606	2,361	2,283	10,155
Simple assault	8	345	701	717	608	569	2,948
Breach of the peace	6	314	942	1,278	1,110	1,038	4,688
Drunkenness	0	11	21	23	29	33	117
Other	2	116	439	588	614	643	2,402
Motor vehicle offences	15	240	884	1,905	2,096	2,293	7,433
Dangerous and careless driving	3	29	141	314	247	230	964
Drunk driving	4	27	95	187	211	235	759
Speeding	0	4	72	219	267	345	907
Unlawful use of vehicle	8	170	475	867	967	1,038	3,525
Vehicle defect offences	0	1	22	128	142	133	426
Other	0	9	79	190	262	312	852

Source: Scottish Office (CCJ Stats) 1998.

A fairly wide range of disposals is available to the courts, even when dealing with young offenders. The fine is the most frequently issued disposal, and young persons under twenty-one who are given time to pay may be placed under the supervision of a person appointed by the court to assist and advise them. The court may ordain the accused to find caution (pronounced "cay-shun") for good behaviour for a period up to one year and in respect of an amount of money considered appropriate by the court. In other words, the offender must surrender the specified amount and be of good behaviour for the specified period in order for the money to be returned. Failure to be of good behaviour will lead to forfeiture of the money.

The offender may be put on probation for a period specified by the court. A more recent option available to courts for sixteen and seventeen year olds is the imposition of a supervised attendance order, supplementary to the imposition of a fine. (Supervised attendance orders were introduced in 1990 as an alternative to imprisonment for fine default). If the offender attends a place of supervision when directed for between ten and 100 hours, the fine is discharged. The offender may pay part of the fine and attend a place of supervision for a proportionately shorter period.

Another alternative to imprisonment is the imposition of a community service order in respect of persons over sixteen, requiring them to undertake unpaid work (normally gardening, helping the elderly or the disabled, etc.) for between 40 and 240 hours under the supervision of an officer of the local authority in which he resides. Offences involving the use of motor vehicles may lead to the disqualification from holding or obtaining a licence to drive a motor vehicle. A compensation order may be imposed instead of or in addition to another disposal, requiring the offender to pay a specified amount of compensation for any personal injury, loss or damage caused, whether directly or indirectly, by the acts which constituted the offence.

For less serious offences, convicted persons may be admonished by the court or, if it appears that the circumstances of the case, the nature of the offence and the character of the offender suggest further punishment is inappropriate, given an absolute discharge (in which case the conviction is quashed).

Table 11
Persons aged under 21 with a charge proved by age and main penalty in Scotland, 1996.

Main penalty				Age			
	<16	16	17	18	19	20	Total
Total	161	2,857	7,201	8,802	8,024	8,122	35,167
Detention of child	40	-	-	-	-	-	40
Young Offenders' Institution	2	374	1,169	1,147	1,008	1,044	4,744
Insane or hospital order	-	2	-	3	2	9	16
Community service order	8	245	564	512	461	453	2,243
Probation	18	523	825	629	500	457	2,952
Fine	13	1,069	3,193	5,088	5,038	5,147	19,548
Compensation order	1	100	156	134	87	89	567
Admonition or caution	23	397	1,188	1,181	828	845	4,462
Remit to Children's Hearing	46	110	35	1	-	-	192
Absolute discharge	5	37	71	107	100	78	398

Source: Scottish Office (CCJ Stats) 1998.

The intention of the Kilbrandon Report had been that young persons aged between sixteen and twenty-one who were accused of criminal offences would be prosecuted before adult criminal courts, and the Juvenile Court system would consequently be abolished. The availability of Children's Hearings does not, however, preclude the appearance of children aged between eight and sixteen before courts, albeit under carefully prescribed conditions, if they are accused of serious crimes and offences. Children under thirteen may only be prosecuted for any offence on the instructions of the Lord Advocate; children aged between thirteen and sixteen may only be prosecuted on the instructions of the Lord Advocate or of Crown Counsel acting on his behalf; and such prosecutions may only be brought before the High Court or a Sheriff Court. In such cases, a copy of the police report to the Procurator Fiscal is sent to the Reporter for information.

Special arrangements are made prior to the court appearance and in courts where cases involving children are to be heard. The Chief Constable of the area in which the offence is alleged to have been committed must send notification of the date, time and nature of the charge to the local council for the area in which the court has jurisdiction. The council is required to prepare and submit to the court background reports concerning the child's school record, health and character. The Procurator Fiscal must notify, where possible, the child's parents or guardian as to the date, time and location of the court hearing, and inform them if they are required to attend court. The Procurator Fiscal must also notify the Sheriff Clerk in time for the necessary arrangements to be made on the day of the child's court appearance. The court in which the diet is to take place must not be in use for at least one hour before and at least one hour after the case is called, in order to prevent an accused child from associating with any accused adults awaiting their own court appearance in respect of other charges. Female accused children must be looked after by a woman while they are in the court.

Children apprehended by the police, with or without a warrant, are brought before a court as soon as possible. If there is likely to be a delay in bringing a child before a court he may be liberated on his or her own undertaking, or that of a parent or guardian, to appear in court on a specified date. The undertaking must be given in writing, signed by the child, parent or guardian and countersigned by a senior police officer. Breach of an undertaking to appear constitutes an offence. In cases where a child is accused of serious offences, where it is deemed necessary to prevent him associating with known criminals, or where it is believed that his liberation could defeat the ends of justice, if a court appearance cannot be arranged quickly the senior police officer must arrange to have the child taken to a place of safety, such as a local authority residential establishment, a community home, a hospital or "other suitable place". If such a place of safety is unavailable, if it is impractical to take the child there, if there are medical grounds which raise concern for the child's health or if the child is considered too unruly for a place of safety, he may be detained in a police station until the court hearing. As with Children's Hearings, press or media reporting of court cases involving children under sixteen is subject to restrictions preventing the publication of the child's name, address, school or details by which he or she may be identified.

If the child pleads guilty to an offence which, if committed by someone aged over twenty-one, could lead to imprisonment, a Sheriff sitting summarily can sentence the child to a period of detention in local authority residential accommodation for up to one year. The ability of the Sheriff to impose detention forthwith indicates a departure from the thinking behind earlier legislation, in which the child's interests were paramount. Whilst this is still normally the case, a child's interests can be outweighed by considerations such as public safety and the preservation of good order.

The local authority would be responsible for the child's welfare as if he or she were under a supervision requirement. The Sheriff may immediately refer the case to the Principal Reporter so that a Children's Hearing may be convened, either to dispose of the case itself or to formulate advice for the Sheriff. If the child is already under supervision the case must be referred to a Children's Hearing. References to Hearings from criminal courts increased from 456 in 1994 to 499 in 1995. Remission of cases for disposal to Hearings from the courts also increased, from 163 in 1994 to 213 in 1995.

If the court remands or commits for trial or sentence a person under twenty-one who has not been released on bail or ordained to appear, there are various options. Children under sixteen may be detained in local authority secure accommodation or a place of safety. Young persons over sixteen or children between fourteen and sixteen who are considered unruly or depraved may be committed to a remand centre for a period, both of which are specified by the court; or a prison if no remand centre is available. Children over fourteen who are detained under local authority care but prove unruly or depraved may be transferred to a remand centre (or, if none is available, to prison). Those already on remand or in prison may be transferred to local authority care if the Sheriff considers remand or prison to be no longer necessary.

The sentencing of children convicted on indictment of a serious or violent offence is governed in part by sections 205, 207 and 208 of the Criminal Procedure (Scotland) Act 1995. Section 205 prescribes sentencing options for murder, and requires children so convicted "to be detained without limit of time and shall be liable to be detained in such place, and under such conditions, as the Secretary of State may direct." When passing sentence, judges may recommend the minimum period which should elapse before the convicted person may be released on licence, and must give reasons for such a recommendation. An appeal may be lodged against the sentence.

Section 207 directs that persons under twenty-one may not be sentenced to imprisonment. Young persons aged between sixteen and twenty-one may be sentenced to a specified period of detention in a Young Offenders' Institution if the judge believes that no other disposal is appropriate and states reasons for such a disposal. Section 208 allows a court to sentence a child who has been convicted on indictment to a specified period of detention if it believes that no other disposal is appropriate, and the child will be liable to be detained in such place and on such conditions as the Secretary of State may direct.

Table 12
Section 205 detainees, by offence, gender and age when convicted

Date of sentence	Offence	Gender	Age when sentenced	Sentence	Time served as of June 1996
Aug 1976	Murder, Assault, Att. robbery, Att. robbery	Male	15	Without limit of time (WLT)	20 years
July 1982	Murder	Male	14	Her Majesty's Pleasure (HMP)	14 years
Jan 1986	Murder	Male	15	WLT	10 years
Sept 1987	Murder	Male	15	HMP	9 years
Sept 1988	Murder	Male	15	WLT	7 years
July 1990	Murder	Female	15	WLT	7 years
July 1991	Murder	Male	15	WLT	5 years

Source: Cutting and Asquith, 1997.

Scottish Office statistics show that the average daily population of young offenders (aged under twenty-one) in penal establishments in Scotland rose from 719 in 1995 to 770 in 1996, and that the total number of receptions of young offenders to penal establishments also rose from 3,986 in 1995 to 4,697 in 1996.

Table 13
Receptions of young offenders to penal establishments by type of custody, 1995-96

Type of custody	1995	1996
Direct sentence	2,772	3,112
In default of fine or compensation order	1,214	1,567
Total receptions	3,986	4,679

Source: Scottish Office Statistical Bulletin "Prison Statistics Scotland, 1996", CrJ/1997/8, Table 7, December 1997.

Table 14
Receptions of young offenders to penal establishments by type of custody and sex, 1996

Type of custody	Male	Female	Total
Direct sentence	3,047	65	3,112
In default of fine or compensation order	1,506	61	1,567
Total receptions	4,553	126	4,679

Source: Scottish Office Statistical Bulletin "Prison Statistics Scotland, 1996", CrJ/1997/8, Table 8, December 1997.

Table 15
Direct receptions of young offenders to penal establishments by age, 1995-96

Age group	1995	1996
15 or under	2	4
16-20	2,770	3,108
Total young offenders	2,772	3,112

Source: Scottish Office Statistical Bulletin "Prison Statistics Scotland, 1996", CrJ/1997/8, Table 13, December 1997.

Table 16
Unruly certificate remands by sex and age, 1995-96

	1995	1996
Total	86	66
Male	84	65
Female	2	·1
14	12	9
15	55	37
16	18	18
17	1	2

Source: Scottish Office Statistical Bulletin "Prison Statistics Scotland, 1996", CrJ/1997/8, Table 22, December 1997.

Table 17
Unruly certificate remands by main crime and offence, 1995-96

	1995	1996
Crimes	81	63
Non-sexual crimes of violence	42	21
Crimes of indecency	2	2
Crimes of dishonesty	29	29
Fire raising, vandalism, etc.	1	3
Other crimes	7	8
Offences	5	3
Miscellaneous offences	2	2
Motor vehicle offences	3	1

Source: Scottish Office Statistical Bulletin "Prison Statistics Scotland, 1996", CrJ/1997/8, Table 23, December 1997.

Bibliography and Further Reading

Asquith, S. (ed.) "Children and Young People in Conflict with the Law", Research Highlights in Social Work 30, London: Jessica Kingsley Publishers, 1996.

Asquith, S. and Samuel, E. "Criminal Justice and Related Services for Young Adult Offenders: A Review", The Scottish Office Central Research Unit, 1994.

Asquith, S., Buist, M., Loughran, N., Macaulay, C. and Montgomery, M. "Children, Young People and Offending in Scotland: A Research Review", The Scottish Office Central Research Unit, 1998

Children (Scotland) Act, 1995 (c.36)

"Children's Hearings", Factsheet No. 7, The Scottish Office Information Directorate, 1993.

Criminal Procedure (Scotland) Act, 1995 (c.46)

Cutting, E. and Asquith S. (with Docherty, M.) "Crimes of Violence: Children who Commit Serious Crimes Including Murder", unpublished paper for Central Research Unit, 1997.

Local Government etc. (Scotland) Act 1994 (c.39)

Social Work (Scotland) Act, 1968 (c.49).

The Kilbrandon Report, "Children and Young Persons Scotland", HMSO, Edinburgh, 1995.

The Scottish Office Statistical Bulletin (Criminal Justice Series), "Criminal Proceedings in Scottish Courts, 1996", CrJ/1998/1, March 1998.

The Scottish Office Statistical Bulletin (Criminal Justice Series), "Prison Statistics Scotland, 1996", CrJ/1997/8, December 1997.

The Scottish Office Statistical Bulletin (Social Work Series), "Referrals of Children to Reporters and Children's Hearings 1995-96", SWK/CH/1997/20, May 1997. (Publication of data on the Children's Hearing system has been taken over by the Scottish Children's Reporter Administration; a report is due by the end of May 1998.)

PRACTICE AND PROCEDURES FOR THE TREATMENT OF YOUNG OFFENDERS IN THE REPUBLIC OF IRELAND

Olwyn Burke, Research Consultant

Introduction

Irish law as regards the treatment of children and young offenders is still governed by the Children's Act of 1908. A very extensive Children's Bill was published in December, 1996, but it is still awaiting Dáil approval, so the 1908 Act remains the principal statute in use for the treatment of children in the Irish Criminal Justice System.

Doli Incapax

The age of criminal responsibility in Ireland is among the lowest in Europe, standing at 7 years of age, although there are intentions to increase it to 10 under the new bill, so that it will be more in line with the rest of Europe. Children between the ages of 7 and 14, to be convicted, must be proved by the prosecution to have known that what they did was wrong.

Garda Treatment of Young Offenders

Policy-making is under-developed in Ireland generally as far as criminological research is concerned, although there have been several initiatives set up in recent years, albeit uncoordinated, to respond more appropriately to current criminological problem areas, including the position of juveniles in the Irish criminal justice system.

In similar vein to the many initiatives already in place elsewhere, the focus recently in Ireland for the Gardaí has been to divert children away from crime and the criminal justice system, towards training and education. The Garda National Juvenile Office was set up in 1991 to deal with all matters concerning juveniles: including developing and researching programmes for diversion, programmes for schools, crime prevention programmes for "at risk" juveniles and also for advancing greater liaison with youths. A number of successful initiatives have been in place to support this diversion away from the criminal justice system. The Garda Juvenile Diversion Programme operates under the supervision and direction of the Garda National Juvenile Office. The Garda Juvenile Diversion Programme, a pre-prosecution scheme aimed at those under 18 years of age and set up as far back as 1963, has the dual aim of preventing first time offenders appearing in court and also of diverting the same offenders away from criminal to legitimate activity.

Under this programme, Garda policy as regards the prosecution of young offenders is not to prosecute unless the gravity of the crime demands it[1]. Instead, cautioning, both formal (which requires that the offence be non-minor in nature and that the caution be administered in the Garda Station by a Superintendent in the presence of the offender and his/her parents) and informal (which requires the offence to be one which is minor in nature and the caution

---

[1] According to both common law police discretion and the 1991 The Policy of An Garda Síochána in Respect of Juvenile Offenders.

to be administered by the local JLO) is widely used to avoid the formal prosecution of the child in court. The total number of juveniles included in the programme since its inception in 1963 up to 1997 is 94,778, with 83% of that total being male and 17% female.

The number of young persons cautioned under the scheme, who therefore consequently avoid prosecution in court for that offence, has actually increased from less than 700 in 1973 to 4,500 in 1991 and further to 12,000 in 1997. In the same year, 1997, only 20% (3,000) of alleged offenders under the age of 18 were deemed unsuitable for the scheme. Homicides are the only crimes which cannot be dealt with under the scheme.

A follow-up scheme of some sort is necessary however in order to fully evaluate the cautioning process.

The total number of referrals to the Juvenile Liaison Office for 1997 was 15,075. This broke down into the following crime-types: 1. Larceny, 21%; 2. Criminal Damage, 16%; 3. Burglary, 12%; 4. Public Order, 7%; 5. Vehicle Offences, 8%; 6. Drink Offences, 9%; 7. Others, 27% (See Figure 1).

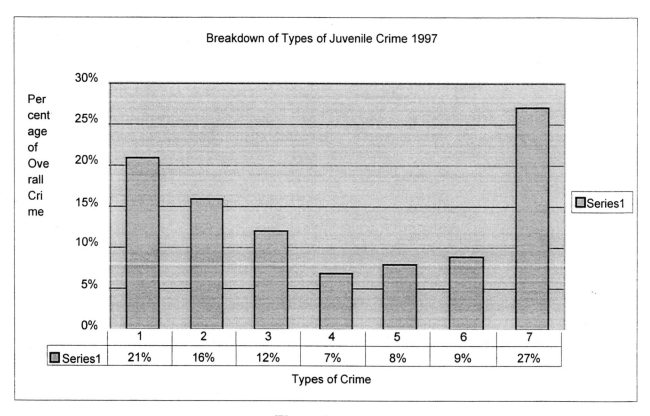

Figure 1

Violent offences also made up the total with 868 common assault offences; 174, serious assault offences; 73, arson; 66, Firearms; 103, Sexual; 76 Assaults and Rapes; 10, Aggravated Burglary.

Court Treatment of Young Offenders

Once a child has been arrested and the decision made that the matter should proceed to court, there are a number of options open to the court with regard to disposals.

The District Court in Ireland, which has its equivalent in England with the Magistrates' Court but with professional judges, has jurisdiction to deal summarily with all indictable offences regarding children, excluding homicides. The only court in Ireland which deals specifically with children is in Dublin, The Children's Court, out-with that, children's proceedings in the District Courts are heard at a different time and a different place to adults and of course proceedings are held in camera.

Disposals

Disposals available to the courts in relation to young offenders are listed under the 1908 Children's Act at s.107. They include:

- Dismissing the charge
- Discharging the offender on his entering into a recognisance
- Charging the offender and placing him under the supervision of a probation officer
- Committing the offender to the care of a relative or other fit person
- Sending the offender to an industrial school
- Ordering the offender to pay a fine, damages or costs
- Ordering the parent or guardian of the offender to give security for his good behaviour
- Committing the offender to custody in a place of detention provided under this part of the Act
- Sentencing him to imprisonment
- Dealing with the case in any other manner in which it may be legally dealt with.

Custody

In Ireland there appears to be a culture of custody for both adults and juveniles who are found guilty before the court of committing a crime. Accommodation in the Institutions and Schools established in the State for young offenders is, however, insufficient to meet demand. In 1993, young offenders under the age of 21 represented an extremely high 29% (1,893) of the total number (6,585) of convicted committals for that year, while those under the age of 17 represented 2.5% (163).

There is only one prison established specifically for offenders aged between 17 and 21 (St. Patrick's Institution) which means that young offenders can be found spread throughout adult prisons. This recourse to adult prisons for these young offenders is unfortunately quite extensive. On rare occasions those aged 15 who are certified as being unruly may be placed in adult prisons where they are segregated from the adult prisoners. Greater variety and flexibility of regimes may be necessary. As it stands now, sentences for young offenders can range from anything from one year to more than two years in adult prisons.

Under the Probation of Offenders Act 1907, a young offender may be conditionally discharged if he/she gives a formal undertaking to be on good behaviour for a certain period and to follow the directions of the supervising Probation Officer.

Under the Criminal Justice Act 1983, community service represents a non-custodial alternative to imprisonment. Offenders in this case must be over the age of 16 and they must also consent to this disposal. The maximum number of hours of community service which can be done is 240.

Effective modernisation of the law governing the treatment of children would be brought about by the proposed legislation and greater co-ordination to properly implement the initiatives already in place would achieve the desired effect.

BIBLIOGRAPHY

The Children's Legal Centre (1997) *The Children's Bill, 1996: Issues and Perspectives,* Collected seminar papers

O'Mahony, P. (1992) The Irish Prison System: European Comparisons, *Irish Criminal Law Journal,* 2,1, pp41-54

O'Mahony, P. (1996) *Criminal Chaos: Seven Crises in Irish Criminal Justice,* Dublin: Round Hall Sweet and Maxwell

O'Malley, T. (1995) *Juvenile Justice in Ireland* in Human Rights in Europe, Dublin: Round Hall

Shanley, P. (1970) The formal cautioning of Juvenile Offenders, *The Irish Jurist,* Winter, 262-279

A BRIEF OVERVIEW OF JUVENILE JUSTICE IN IRELAND

Dr. Paul O'Mahony, Irish Penal Reform Trust, Ireland

Introduction

The submission of the Children's Legal Centre to the National Crime Forum (1998) summarised the present parlous state of the Irish juvenile justice system in the following terms:

"Over the past two decades, the Irish system of juvenile justice has attracted considerable criticism regarding the archaic nature of many of its provisions: the lack of suitable secure accommodation for young offenders, in particular young female offenders; the lack of a comprehensive spectrum of community based alternatives to corrective institutionalisation; the lack of any innovative thinking regarding the issue; and the fragmented nature of the current system of juvenile justice...The current system of juvenile justice, with the exception of a number of minor new measures, is rooted in early 20th century conceptualisation of childhood and a philosophy of justice which is in the main viewed as unacceptable in a society, where a respect for the rights of the child and protection for children is increasingly viewed as desirable...Such stagnation has manifested itself in terms of a lack of any form of statutory response to a patently ineffective, costly (both to the child and the state) and archaic system, which currently offers little justice to those who are deemed to have violated the spectrum of activities that are considered worthy of punishment."

Social deprivation and youth crime and drug abuse

The Republic of Ireland is a small jurisdiction of about 3.8 million people with a relatively low and comparatively manageable crime problem. In 1995, the figures for reported indictable crime peaked at 102,000, the highest level in the history of the state. However, these levels are quite low by European standards, and indeed are about a half to a third of those in most Western European countries. It is worth noting that Dublin, with a population of about 1 million, has about 60 per cent of all crime in the country. In the last two years, the indictable crime figures have fallen substantially and now stand at just over 90,000. Currently, at any one time there are about 2,500 prisoners in custody in the state. This is a moderate detention level by European standards, but it masks a high imprisonment rate. At present there are a very large number of offenders sent to prison on brief stays for fine defaulting and a large number released very early due to the pressures on prison accommodation. There are presently plans to expand the prison system to about 4,000 places by the year 2002, and these places are expected to be filled immediately.

There is only a small body of research and analytic work on juvenile delinquency and the operation of the juvenile justice system in Ireland. However, large scale, longitudinal research projects in other countries have established fairly conclusively that parental neglect or rejection, lack of discipline or inconsistent discipline, adult modeling of criminal behaviours and advocacy of anti-social attitudes, peer pressure, school failure, and material want and boredom, can all play an important role in promoting juvenile delinquency and should be regarded as significant risk factors. It is also well established by research in Britain and other developed Western countries that 16 to 18 are the peak years for criminal offending and that nearly half of all crime is committed by teenagers. The international literature also indicates that many teenagers from all sorts of backgrounds experiment with minor delinquent behaviour, including crimes of dishonesty, aggression and vandalism. But the group who go on to have a serious criminal career are a small minority, which is not by any means representative of teenagers as a whole or even of teenagers of the lower social classes. As the Cambridge Delinquency Study (West and Farrington 1973) has convincingly shown, children from a small number of particularly troublesome, dysfunctional families account for a large proportion of relatively serious teenage crime.

Juvenile Delinquency in Ireland

Although we lack comprehensive research data on the issues in Ireland, there is enough evidence to justify the belief that the generalisations and analyses about the wellsprings of juvenile crime found in the international research literature are equally applicable to the case of Irish juvenile delinquency. There are important individual factors, related to temperament, personality, academic ability and personal history that play a vital role in the genesis of serious repeat offending, but there can be little doubt that family, interpersonal and broader social and economic factors also play a leading role. As will be argued, there is some reason to believe that highly concentrated forms of social deprivation and an opiate drugs epidemic that has afflicted the most deprived areas of Dublin since 1980 have an especially powerful influence on delinquency and youth crime in Ireland. Although these factors interact with the other causal factors, it is likely they also have a independent criminogenic effect.

An Inter-Departmental Group has recently produced a report on "Urban Crime and Disorder" (1992), which focused on young people in trouble with the law in Irish cities. This report was stimulated by riots in some of the impoverished suburbs of West Dublin. These riots were a particularly severe illustration of the underlying hostility between the police and youth gangs in many of the deprived areas in Irish cities. In these areas, there is a major problem with so-called joy-riding and many people have been killed in joy-riding 'accidents', both perpetrators and innocent bystanders. There is also a growing problem with public order offences and vandalism; for example, the incidence of arson and of malicious damage to schools has greatly increased in recent years. The Inter-Departmental Group's report concluded that

> "failure to assign essential resources to the task of dealing with factors which contribute towards urban crime and disorder could have extremely serious and expensive consequences for Irish society as a whole in the longer-term".

131

This report is important because it marks a turning point in social policy, involving a new official readiness to acknowledge both the role of social deprivation in the genesis of crime and the responsibility of government to implement effective programmes to combat the problem.

The Inter-Departmental Group identified crucial, socio-economic contributory factors - e.g. poverty and lack of educational and employment opportunities - that can and must be tackled, if the rising trend in juvenile crime and urban disorder is to be halted and reversed. These broadly defined socio-economic disadvantages are, of course, compounded by other widely prevalent, family-based and individualised ills, noted by the Inter-Departmental Group, such as "alcoholism in the home, juvenile alcohol and drug abuse, poor parenting, including child abuse and neglect, lack of self-esteem, boredom and truancy". Irish research has been unequivocal in identifying poverty, low social status, school failure, family disruption and large family size as characteristics of young offenders and suggests that persistent serious offending may be associated with quite small, circumscribed communities of especially disadvantaged families to an even greater extent than in Britain (O'Mahony, 1985, 1997).

A Thriving Drug Culture

Currently in Dublin, an opiate drugs subculture is endemic in almost all of the severely socio-economically deprived districts. Research has indicated that children as young as twelve years of age in these areas start on intravenous heroin use (O'Mahony, 1997). It is estimated that in Dublin there are between 6,000 and 10,000 heroin addicts, many of them teenagers. Apart from the criminal conduct intrinsic to drug use, the heroin epidemic in Dublin has spawned a great deal of property crime and violence. Organised crime has flourished in Ireland, reaping vast illicit rewards from the importation and distribution of heroin, ecstasy and cannabis. Young people using hard drugs are inevitably drawn in large numbers into crime, especially mugging, shop-lifting, robbery and burglary aimed at raising funds for the purchase of drugs.

A recent study (Keogh, 1997) estimated that 91 per cent of drug users in Dublin obtain money from crime and that the typical age of first contact with the police was 15 years. This study also estimated that drug users were responsible for 66 per cent of all detected indictable crime in Dublin and over 80 per cent of all burglaries, robberies and thefts from cars. On average, drug users committed three times as much crime as non-drug using criminals. Of the group studied, 27 per cent were under 21 years of age; per cent had left school without qualifications (37% leaving before the legally permitted age); and 73 per cent had begun drug use before the age of 18. The two commonest categories chosen as reasons for starting with drugs were "I was curious about it" (45%) and "I was put under pressure to try it" (16%). Eighty per cent stated they had a poor or no understanding of the effects of drugs when they began using. Only three per cent of the users were employed, but they spent an average of £96 per day on drugs, indicating the extent of the drug-related, economic drive behind their criminal activity.

General Motives for Juvenile Crime

A simplified but plausible summary of the motives for much juvenile crime is that it is committed for reasons of material gain, self-esteem, prestige amongst peers or for pure excitement. All of these motives have an important social dimension and are strongly influenced by social contingencies. While it is theoretically possible for parents, who live in very deprived areas, to insulate their children entirely from the surrounding culture, it is very difficult for them to do so. Most children growing up in a deprived city area will be exposed to and powerfully influenced by a strong and vibrant, local youth culture. In some areas of Dublin in particular, the local youth culture perceives drug use as an exciting and attractive lifestyle option, offering not only pleasurable diversion and subjective escape from a bleak environment but also readily achievable role models for material and financial success and membership of a self-affirming 'anti-community'.

Poverty and harsh conditions of deprivation place families under significant stress and can undermine the ability and capacity of parents to provide the kind of environment which fosters pro-social behaviour and sound moral development. However, even children who have been well socialized in a conventional way within the family are open to being influenced and persuaded by peer-groups and the powerful subculture surrounding them. This is especially the case if the subculture involves hard drug-taking. Opiate drug use has proven to be very seductive to all sorts of young people from deprived backgrounds. This is undoubtedly due to the fact that the undeserved experience of harsh conditions and of a stigmatised inferior social role leads directly to disaffection, anger, boredom and lack of self-esteem, and psychologically prepares the ground for both crime and drug addiction. Drug use, once established, imposes its own exacting and often criminal imperatives on the addicted.

While individual and family factors: such as an impulsive temperament; low intelligence; poor parental discipline; and the inculcation of anti-social attitudes by criminal fathers or siblings greatly increase the risk of serious, persistent delinquent behaviour and drug use, it is necessary to acknowledge that they are not necessary preconditions for delinquency in deprived areas, where delinquent and drug abusing gangs abound. Opiate addiction, amongst lower social class youths, clearly entails a high risk of serious criminal involvement independent of other individual and interpersonal risk factors for delinquency. Furthermore, in marginalised communities, which see themselves as unfairly excluded, the genesis of juvenile delinquency and crime is sometimes less in the failure of socialisation or in a 'criminal personality' than in the fact that the normative moral values of mainstream society are actively rejected by the local peer group and replaced by a different code that tolerates or encourages certain types of criminal activity.

In short, deprivation and disadvantage operate in various and complex ways to foster juvenile delinquency and youth crime. However, in Ireland over the last two decades, the most obvious and most important influence of social deprivation and disadvantage on crime has been through the promotion of opiate drug addiction amongst the young in marginalised areas. It is justifiable to strongly emphasize the role of social deprivation in Ireland because of evidence that Ireland has marked, persistent and particularly severe disparities between the poor and better off sectors of society and because of evidence that the opiate abuse problem is concentrated almost exclusively in the areas of high social deprivation. Ireland has high levels of child poverty and, according to the National Anti-poverty Strategy (1996), children have a 28 per cent risk (compared with an 18% risk for adults) of belonging to a household with less than half of the average income. Ireland is also one of the most polarised of Western societies with respect to personal wealth and a recent UN study of developed nations indicated that only in the U.S. was there a greater gulf between the poorest and the wealthiest members of society. Indeed, recent economic analysis has indicated that the four budgets of the Irish Government, up to and including 1997, did nothing to alleviate social inequity, but, on the contrary, clearly favoured the better off. Social mobility, especially through the education system is very limited for the most disadvantaged sectors of Irish society and it is estimated that less than 1 per cent of university students are the children of unskilled manual workers, who form about 15 per cent of the population.

New Responses to Social Deprivation and drugs

On the other hand, in the last few years in Ireland, partly in response to the growing awareness of the role of drug abuse in crime and of the contribution of social and economic factors to both crime and drug abuse, more official attention has been paid to the drugs problem and to the problems of social exclusion. As a result, more resources have been directed at the drugs problem and at the structural problems and deficits of highly disadvantaged areas. A National Anti-Poverty Strategy has been published (1996) and an agenda for confronting disadvantage has been established. The Ministerial Task Force on Measures to Reduce the Demand for Drugs has also produced two important reports (1996 & 1997) and helped stimulate a more realistic approach to the drugs problem and a far better level of government funding for the area.

However, it should be noted that the greater official acknowledgement of the problem was also partly driven by a powerful community activist/vigilante anti-drugs movement, which flourished in Dublin through 1996 and 1997. This movement used mass public protest, the patrolling of streets and the eviction of alleged drug dealers from the community area, in order to impinge on the political consciousness and to ameliorate the climate and quality of life in previously drug-infested areas. Partly in response to the anti-drugs community movement, Drugs Task Forces have been set up in 13 areas on a collaborative partnership model, based on joint action between statutory bodies and voluntary and community groups. Many early intervention, treatment, educational, training and rehabilitative initiatives have been instigated or more effectively resourced under the new programmes.

Another major part of the reinvigorated official response has been a redirection of police efforts towards controlling the heroin problem in inner city areas, particularly open dealing and using (the police had previously neglected this problem, choosing to target heroin users for their non-drug crimes only). Operation Dochas was begun in 1996 and placed about 500 additional police on the streets of the drug-infested areas. A large investment has also been made in expanding methadone maintenance treatment programmes. There is now a political commitment to providing such treatment for all those who seek it. However, treatment centres of all kinds have continued to report a growth in the number of new contacts and a continuing flow of teenage clients - indicating that many young people are still being attracted into opiate drug use (O'Higgins 1996).

There has also been a considerably increased investment in recent years in youth activities projects, sports facilities for the young and supportive, educational and training programmes, aimed at prevention and breaking the cycle of educational disadvantage and social exclusion. The Department of Education is experimenting with Head Start type programmes, after school homework clubs in schools in disadvantaged areas, and teacher/counsellors who liaise with parents and attend the home to help at risk children with their studies. The Department of Education also runs Youthreach in 60 centres. This is a full time programme for 15-18 year old early school leavers, which focuses on personal development, skills training and preparation for work. The Department of Enterprise, Trade and Employment runs a similar scheme in 45 centres. Both schemes are targeted at the more than 1,000 children who drop out of school each year before the school-leaving age and so are at special risk of involvement in crime and drug misuse. The Garda Síochána, through its Community Relations Section, administers a total of 14 Department of Justice funded Special Projects. These projects are targeted specifically on at risk youngsters in deprived areas and "endeavour to divert their energies from anti-social activities".

The Juvenile Courts and Penal System

The District Court (equivalent to the Magistrate's Court in England, but presided over by a professional judge) has jurisdiction to deal summarily with a child or young person charged with an indictable offence other than homicide. When dealing with children, the District Court must sit at a different time or in a different place than when dealing with adults. This is generally a matter of a different time, because only Dublin has a separate, dedicated Children's Court. The age of criminal responsibility in Ireland at present is seven. However, it is not in law permitted to imprison anyone under the age of 15. Children, however, may be sent to a reformatory or an industrial school (now both called special schools) operated under the auspices of the Department of Education.

It is also possible for a judge to commit a child offender to the care of a relative or other fit person or to levy a fine, costs and damages from the parent of a young offender. There are no available statistics on the frequency of recourse to these alternative sanctions. Children of 15 may only be sent to prison, if a court issues a certificate that the young person is "unruly or depraved" but this is a relatively rare event. There is one pre-prosecution diversion scheme in the Irish system, aimed specifically at juvenile offenders under 18 years of age. This, the Juvenile Liaison Scheme, is run by the Garda Síochána and involves a formal or informal caution and a period of supervision. Acceptance by the scheme is conditional on the offender admitting the offence and on a degree of cooperation from the offender's family. This scheme has grown greatly in recent years, and, in 1997, there were 12,000 referrals handled, up from about 3,000 in 1990. In 1997, 20 per cent of alleged offenders under 18 years coming to the notice of the Garda Síochána were deemed unsuitable for the cautioning scheme and so were forwarded to be dealt with by the courts. This amounted to a total of approximately 3,000 young people.

The police provide national statistics on the age of persons convicted or against whom the charge was held proved or order made without conviction. In 1997, there were a total of 15,888 such persons. This figure refers to people facing charges for offences committed in both 1997 and previous years. However, they can be examined against the background of a total, in 1997, of 90,875 reported offences, 38,943 detected offences, and 30,767 offences, in which criminal proceedings were commenced. Of the 15,888 convicted persons, then, 6,920, or 44 per cent, were under 21 years of age and 1,538, or 10 per cent were under 17 years of age. Of those under 17 years, 105, or 7 per cent, were female. It can be assumed that many of the 3000 or so cases referred annually to the courts by the Juvenile Liaison Scheme are included in the 44 per cent of convictees under 21 years.

The Success of the Garda Juvenile Liaison Scheme

It is clear that, over recent years, the Garda's Juvenile Liaison pre-prosecution diversion programme has come to play an increasingly central and significant role in the official response to young offenders. The scheme has grown greatly - in 1980, there were 1366 informal and formal cautions of young people under the scheme; in 1990, 3180; and in 1997, 8,583 (17% were of girls, whereas only about 5% of convictions and 2% of those imprisoned in Ireland are female). Along with preventative and rehabilitative community action projects, Probation and Welfare Service hostels for youths; probation supervision; and (for those of 16 and above) Community Service Orders, the scheme constitutes the non-custodial treatment of young offenders in Ireland. In fact, the scheme handles the bulk of cases dealt with, but the question remains whether or not this activity is concentrated almost exclusively on the broad band of less serious delinquent conduct. The Garda claim great success for this scheme, stating that since its inception, 89 per cent of all those cautioned have reached the age of 18 without being prosecuted for a criminal offence. There is a clear need, however, for independent evaluation of the scheme and for a more realistic length of follow-up. Also, there should be specific evaluation of the scheme's effectiveness with young people who qualify as at serious risk of a persistent criminal career.

Nonetheless, this is a very valuable scheme that has the potential for development so as to include more active participation by community and social workers and the offender's family. Indeed, at present the juvenile diversion programme is beginning experiments with the innovative, family conference approach, pioneered in New Zealand. This is a very constructive development. However, one serious problem has emerged already because a decision has been made to appoint the Garda Juvenile Liaison Officer as the facilitator to the conference. Experience elsewhere has demonstrated that this is inappropriate and unworkable since the Garda have an important role in the conference as the agents of law enforcement. Juvenile liaison officers themselves are aware that the facilitator should be and should be seen to be a neutral figure, probably from the local community.

The Juvenile Liaison Office provide a breakdown of the type of crime for which juvenile referrals were made to them, including those cautioned and those referred on to the courts. In 1997 there were 15,075 offences (which broke down in the following way: Larceny 21%;

Criminal Damage 16%; Burglary 12%; Public Order 7%; Vehicle Offences 8%; Drink Offences 9%; Other Miscellaneous 27%). The total included a number of violent offences: 886 cases of common assault and 174 cases of serious assault; 73 cases of arson; 66 firearms offences; 103 sexual offences, including 76 sexual assaults and rapes; and 10 cases of aggravated burglary. Perhaps surprisingly, given the hugely important role of drugs in youth crime in Dublin, the total involved only 486 drug-related offences (413 for possession and 73 for sale or supply). This amounted to 3 per cent of the total number of offences by those under 18 years.

Custodial and Prison Population

One of the most obvious symptoms of the failure of the Irish state to develop progressive policies and practices to deal with the problem of juvenile delinquency is the fact that Ireland has the largest proportion of its prison places taken up by people under 21 years of any country in Western Europe (O'Mahony, 1992). In fact, between 1987 and 1991, 243 children aged 15 and 16, who are not normally imprisonable, were classed as unruly and depraved by the courts and committed to Mountjoy Prison, an overcrowded, drug-infested adult prison, which, to put it mildly, is an extremely unsuitable environment for them. In 1993, there were, in Ireland, a total of 6,585 committals to prison on conviction and 1,893 of these were aged under 21 (29%) and 163 (2.5%) were aged under 17.

For many years, almost a third of the Irish prison population detained at any one time has been under 21. This is about twice the English level, which itself is one of the highest in Europe (although the disparity is somewhat attenuated by the greater proportion of under 21 year olds in the Irish general population). The most recent figures do indicate a decline in the proportion of under 21s in prison and in 1998 they constitute less than 25 per cent of the total prison population or about 600 individuals. There are two prisons (designated as Places of Detention) dedicated to those under aged 17 to 20 years - St Patrick's Institution (about 200 places) and Shanganagh Castle, an Open Centre (about 44 places). The modern prison, Wheatfield, has some units designated for juveniles, who are to an extent kept apart from adults (up to 100 places out of 340). However, juvenile prisoners are distributed throughout the prison system and considerable numbers can be found in adult prisons. Some European jurisdictions have ended imprisonment for those under 21 except for the most unusual cases. The fact that Ireland continues to imprison young people at such a high rate in what is frequently a highly criminogenic environment for young people, is a serious sign of the lack of progress in this area. It points to a failure to come up with or to utilise more positive and constructive sanctions for young people based on community service, training, education and family support.

Compared with the wide use of Juvenile Liaison cautions for those under 18 years and the use of imprisonment for those under 21 years, the Probation and Welfare Service handles a surprisingly small number of juvenile cases per annum. In 1993, they supervised 687 people of between 16 and 20 years on Community Service Orders. In the same year, they supervised 159 people under 16 years and 400 people between 16 and 20 years of age on Probation Orders; 127, under 16 years, and 340, between 16 and 20 years of age, during a period of deferment of penalty.

Therefore, the Probation and Welfare Service had direct supervisory contact with 286 people under 16 years and 1,427 people aged between 16 and 20 years of age. The Probation and Welfare Service, often in collaboration with community groups, also runs some hostels and workshop training places for young offenders, who are under their supervision. In 1993, 18 males under 16 and 37 males between 16 and 20 years on supervision from the courts and a further 17 on release from custody took up residence in the hostels. In 1993, Training Workshops had a total throughput of 280, perhaps a majority of whom were aged over 18 years.

While the Probation and Welfare Service supervision and the Prison system, in about equal measure, are relied on as the main responses to those juvenile offenders over 16 years, who have not been deemed to qualify for the cautioning scheme, those under 16 years (or under 17 years for females) who are considered to require custodial or residential care are largely the responsibility of the Department of Education. There are six institutions run by the Department of Education for the assessment, the safe custody and the reform of young people in trouble with the law. They are St Michael's Assessment Centre and St Laurence's Special School in Dublin, St Joseph's, Clonmel, an industrial school, the Boy's and Girl's Oberstown Schools, both reformatories, and the highly secure reformatory, Trinity House. The latter three institutions are on a single site, a few miles north of Dublin.

In total, these institutions provide a maximum of 226 places (only 15 for girls). They are by no means sufficient to meet the demand. There is currently a huge problem with the provision of appropriate institutions for youngsters in trouble with the law or at risk. Judges frequently find themselves at a loss for a residential place for an at risk or out of control youngster and have been vocal in their criticism of the current provision. In Dublin, there is a very serious problem with homeless youth who often drift into crime and drug use. Provision for them is far from satisfactory and until recently many of those who came to official attention or sought help ended up staying in bed and breakfast accommodation without any supervision. There is a need for far more residential places for both boys and girls and for far more variability and flexibility in the type of regimes on offer. At present a number of high and moderate security units (7) and high support units (12), the former intended to hold 6 young people, the latter 5, are planned or in the process of being built. These units will each have a staff of 17 and be under the control of the eight local Irish Health Boards. This plan reflects recent High Court decisions that the Health Boards are under a Constitutional obligation to provide appropriate residential care for children who need to be detained for their own welfare.

However, lack of data, informed analysis and coordinated forward planning in this area are a severe problem. There has been little monitoring of the performance of the current institutions and little research on the whole issue of present and future requirements in terms of both number of places, types of places (ie. required levels of security and the correct balance between security and a supportive, habilitation/rehabilitation ethos) and optimal service provision. This lack of research needs to be urgently addressed. A Scottish expert, Mr Hugh Laxton, who recently completed a report for the Irish Government on this area, pointed out that even the planned new provisions are unlikely to work, because of the poor level of provision in the general child care area, including crucially the failure to implement and fully resource the provisions of the Child Care Act 1991. There is a lack of ordinary residential units and hostels for children who do not, or no longer, need high support or high security. There is also a severe lack of foster care for children (at 31st December 1997 there were 3,113 children in foster care in the state) and a generally underdeveloped foster care system, although the Child Care (Placement of Children in Foster Care) Regulations, 1995 strengthen the position of foster parents in relation to the removal of children from their care and place a new stress on the need for development of 'care plans' for foster children. Laxton summarised the shortcomings of the current system in the following terms:

"The conclusion to be drawn from this review of current policies and practices is that dysfunctional and inadequate families are being cared for by dysfunctional and inadequate services ...some children being brought into care are being inadequately cared for and in some instances further damaged by the experiences. Many of the children subject to judicial review and/or causing concern to Health Boards and residential schools have been known to the care services for a long time and their problems have been invariably exacerbated by a series of inappropriate placements".

Perhaps part of the official reluctance to get to grips with the problem of institutional care for young people who come to the attention of the courts derives from the very negative experience with the experimental 'Children's Prison' for 12 to 16 year olds at Loughan House, Co. Cavan, which was under the control of the Department of Justice. This prison, set up in the early eighties, was abandoned after a few years, having been subjected to a barrage of vociferous criticism from some sectors of the public for the years of its existence. Unfortunately, no research has been done on this, in Irish terms, innovative and quite well-resourced institution and on why it was considered a failure. Some very necessary and useful lessons have, therefore, not been learnt. It is well known, however, that quite a number of the children who graduated from Loughan House quickly went on to establish very serious criminal careers, which included murder in more than one case.

New Juvenile Justice Legislation

One of the most notable initiatives in the juvenile justice area in recent years is the Children Bill, first published in 1996. The Children Bill is long overdue since much of the legislation in this area dates from the beginning of the century and from the 1908 British Children Act, which has long ago been replaced in Britain. Among other things, the current Children Bill raises the age of criminal responsibility from 7 years to 10; defines a child as a "person under the age of 18 years unless the context otherwise requires"; proposes a set of procedures to govern police interviewing of juveniles; puts the Juvenile Liaison Scheme onto a statutory footing and provides for it to run family conferences; allows for curfews on juveniles (Restriction on Movement Orders); proposes the setting up of Day Centres, which would provide purposeful occupation and programmes for delinquent youth and the use by the courts of Day Centre Orders; proposes that compensation be levied from parents of delinquent children; advances physical designs and legal structures for a more child-centred court system; proposes to abolish the present system of industrial and reformatory schools and replace it with a system of Child Detention Centres for children under 17 years, which will operate under a single Board of

Management; proposes to grant the Health Boards powers to detain, under special care orders, non-offending children (who are behaviourally at risk or in need of care and protection) in secure high support units, however without the 'due process' safeguards of the criminal justice system; and proposes the curtailment of the current discretion of the management of special schools to refuse to take in a child, either because of accommodation pressures or the unsuitability of the child. In other words, the Bill is a rather confusing mixum-gatherum of concepts and proposals gleaned from numerous contemporary sources and proposed responses to some of the more pressing, current, practical problems. In Ireland in the juvenile justice area, caring interventions - which tend to be under-resourced - presently coexist uneasily with unmodified, harsh, blaming approaches - which are borrowed from the adult criminal justice system and tend to be far better resourced. The new proposed legislation suggests a major but probably unworkable shift of moral and criminal blame from children onto their parents without fully resolving the underlying inadequacies, contradictions and paradoxes of the current situation.

While more responsible parenting is a fitting and right aim for our society, it is hardly justifiable or feasible to promote better parenting through the punishment and coercion of parents of delinquent children and by the means of an inevitably crude and lumbering criminal justice system. Many parents of at risk children have poor material and psychological resources and require substantial assistance and support to improve their parenting skills rather than punishment for their lack of them. The Children Bill is at best a half-hearted attempt to bring practice in this area in line with modern concepts. It fails to resolve the conflict between caring or welfare approaches and controlling or justice approaches. However, it is a step in the direction of reform, does achieve some needed improvements, such as in the raised age of criminal responsibility, and does offer the chance for a more coordinated, more child-sensitive, more child-directed and more welfare-based approach. If properly implemented, it also promises better facilities and resources in certain areas, such as the courts and, more generally, a greater investment in the whole area of juvenile justice. The present status of the Children Bill is, however, uncertain since the 1997 change of government. It is likely to undergo some amendment before enactment, but so far the new government has been silent on the issue.

In general terms, the area of juvenile justice, unlike most other areas of the criminal justice and penal systems, is one where there is very considerable public and professional interest and commitment in Ireland. However, this level of concern has not been matched by a corresponding interest and dynamism on the part of the relevant authorities. Public interest does mean that there is an on-going level of research and analysis in the area by various, usually un-funded, isolated, interested parties - for example, professionals working in the area and post-graduate students.

However, the problems in this area, i.e. the seriousness of the phenomenon of juvenile crime, the inadequacies of the institutional and societal response to it, and the cardinal role of social deprivation and drug abuse in the genesis of much youth crime, are so complex and multi-faceted that the current level of information, research, and analysis remains far from sufficient. There are still major gaps in basic information let alone in the development of new thinking. The lack of a coherent and cumulative body of data and analysis means that policy-making in this area tends to be under- or undeveloped and where it does exist, it is often based on untested and unsound assumptions. In recent years there has been a junior Minister with responsibility for children and with a brief that covers justice, education and health. This is a positive step that offers some hope for a more coordinated and focused response in the future. The very welcome new emphasis on and more realistic funding of community-based, partnership approaches and preventative and rehabilitation initiatives to tackle drug abuse, poverty, educational disadvantage and lack of opportunity also demand that the processes of data collection, social policy analysis, service co-ordination and project evaluation be urgently prioritised.

References

Children's Legal Centre (1998) *Submission to the National Crime Forum*

Keogh, E. (1997) *Illicit Drug Use and related criminal activity in the Dublin Metropolitan Area* Templemore: Garda Research Unit

Ministerial Task Force on Measures to Reduce the Demand for Drugs (Rabbite Committee), First (1996) and Second (1997) Reports Dublin: Stationery Office

National Anti-Poverty Strategy (1996) Dublin: Stationery Office

O'Mahony, P. Cullen, R. and O'Hora, H. (1985) *Some Family Characteristics of Irish Juvenile Offenders,* Economic and Social Review (17,1)

O'Mahony, P. (1992) The Irish Prison System: European Comparisons, *Irish Criminal Law Journal*, 2,1, pp41-54

O'Mahony, P. (1996) *Criminal Chaos: Seven Crises in Irish Criminal Justice,* Dublin: Round Hall Sweet and Maxwell

O'Mahony, P. (1997) *Mountjoy Prisoners: A Sociological and Criminological Profile,* Dublin: Stationery Office

O'Higgins, K. (1996) *Treated Drug Misuse in the Greater Dublin Area: Review of Five Years 1990-94* Dublin: Health Research Board

Report of the Interdepartmental Group (1992) *Urban Crime and Disorder,* Dublin: The Stationery Office

West, D. and Farrington, D. (1973) *Who becomes delinquent?* London: Heinemann

A Selective Bibliography on Irish Juvenile Justice

Bowden, M. (1998) *Evaluation of the Copping On Project,* Children's Research Centre: Trinity College Dublin

Burke, H., Carney, C. and Cooke, G. (eds) (1981) *Youth and Justice,* Dublin: Turoe Press

The Children's Legal Centre (1997) *The Children's Bill, 1996: Issues and Perspectives,* Collected seminar papers

The Children's Legal Centre (1997) *Secure Accommodation in Child Care,* Collected seminar papers

Bowden, M. (1998) *Evaluation of the Copping On Project*, Children's Research Centre: Trinity College Dublin

Council for Social Welfare (1991) *The Rights of the Child: Irish Perspectives on the UN Convention* Dublin

Dail Eireann (1992) *Juvenile Crime: Its Causes and its remedies,* First Report of the Select Committee on Crime

Farrelly, J. (1989) *Crime, Custody and Community - Juvenile Justice and Crime with particular relevance to Sean McDermott St.* Dublin: Voluntary and Statutory Bodies

Ferguson, H. and Kenny, P. (1995) *On behalf of the Child: Child Welfare, Child Protection and the Child Care Act 1991,* Dublin

Flynn, A., McDonald, N. and O'Doherty, E. (1967) *A survey of boys in St. Patrick's Institution,* The Irish Jurist Vol. 2

Gilligan, R. (1991) *Irish Child Care Services: Policy, Practice and Provision,* Dublin: Institute of Public Administration

Hannon, D. and Riain, S. (1993) *Pathways to adulthood in Ireland. Causes and consequences of success and failure in transitions amongst Irish youth,* Paper 161 Economic and Social Research Institute Dublin

Hart, I. (1968) *The social and psychological characteristics of institutionalized young offenders in Ireland,* Administration, Vol. 16

Hart, I. (1970) *A survey of some delinquent boys in an Irish industrial school and reformatory,* Economic and Social Review 1, pp182-214

Hart, I. (1974) *Factors relating to reconviction among young Dublin probationers,* Dublin: ESRI

Hart, I. and McQuaid, P. (1974) *Empirical classification of types among delinquent referrals to a child guidance clinic,* Economic and Social Review 5, 2, pp163-173

Henchy Report (1974) Interdepartmental Committee on mentally ill and maladjusted persons *Provision of treatment for juvenile offenders and potential juvenile offenders* Dublin: Stationery Office

Irish Penal Reform Trust (1997) *Is Penal Reform Possible?* A collection of seminar papers, Dublin: IPRT

The Kennedy Report (1970) Committee on Reformatory and Industrial School Systems Dublin: Stationery Office

McVerry, P (1985) *Spike Island: the answer to what?* Dublin: Resource Publications

National Youth Federation (1996) *What Justice for Young People?* Dublin: Irish Youthwork Press

O'Cinnéide, S. (1981) 'The young offender' in McLoone, J. (ed) *The Offender and the Community,* The Social Study Conference

O'Connor, J. (1963) *The Young Offender,* Studies 71

O'Gorman, N. and Barnes, J. (1995) *A Survey of Juvenile Delinquents at St Michael's Assessment Centre,* Dublin: The Chamber of Commerce

O'Mahony, P. Cullen, R. and O'Hora, H. (1984) *Some Family Characteristics of Irish Juvenile Offenders,* Economic and Social Review (17,1)

O'Mahony, P., Murphy, P. and O'Mahony, D. (1982) The Validity of the HDHQ with Juvenile Offenders, *Irish Journal of Psychology* (5,3) pp 185-195

O'Malley, T. (1995) *Juvenile Justice in Ireland* in Human Rights in Europe, Dublin: Round Hall

Osborough, N. (1975) *Borstal in Ireland,* Dublin: Institute of Public Administration

O'Sullivan, E. (1996) *Juvenile Justice in the Republic of Ireland: Future Priorities,* Irish Social Worker, 14

O'Sullivan, D. (1974) *Pre-existing acquaintance and friendship amongst industrial school boys,* Social Studies 3, pp13-23

O'Sullivan, D. (1979) *Case study in an Irish Industrial School: Organisational socialisation and the management of imported identities,* Social Studies, 6, pp265-313

Powell, F. (1995) Deconstructing Juvenile Justice: A Postmodern Policy Dilemma Administration 43

Power, B. (1971) *The Young Lawbreaker,* Social Studies Oct 1971

Quin, M. (1998) *Copping On,* Dublin: Youthreach

Report of the Interdepartmental Group 1992 *Urban Crime and Disorder,* Dublin: The Stationery Office

Ring, M. (1991) Custodial Treatment for Young Offenders, *Irish Criminal Law Journal*, 1

Shanley, P. (1970) The formal cautioning of Juvenile Offenders, *The Irish Jurist*, Winter, 262-279

Task Force on Child Care Services (1980) Final Report Dublin: Stationery Office

CRU RESEARCH - PUBLICATIONS LIST FROM 1999

Poor Housing and Ill Health: A Summary of Research Evidence: Housing Research Branch. (1999) (£2.50)

One Stop Shop Arrangements for Development Related Local Authority Functions: Centre for Planning Research, School of Town and Regional Planning, University of Dundee. (1999) (£5.00)
Summary available: Development Department Research Findings No.63

Research on Walking: System Three. (1999) (£5.00)

Resolving Neighbour Disputes Through Mediation in Scotland: Centre for Criminological and Legal research, University of Sheffield. (1999) (£4.00)
Summary available: Development Department Research Findings No.64

Literature Review of Social Exclusion: Centre for Urban and Regional Studies, University of Birmingham. (1999) (£5.00)

Mentally Disordered Offenders and Criminal Proceedings: Dr M Burman, Department of Sociology and Ms C Connelly, School of Law, University of Glasgow. (1999) (£7.50)

Evaluation of Experimental Bail Supervision Schemes: Ewen McCaig and Jeremy Hardin, MVA Consultancy. (1999) (£6.00)
Summary available: Social Work Research Findings No.28

An Evaluation of the 1997/98 Keep Warm This Winter Campaign: Simon Anderson and Becki Sawyer, System 3. (1999) (£5.00)
Summary available: Social Work Research Findings No.29

Attitudes Towards Crime, Victimisation and the Police in Scotland: A Comparison of White and Ethnic Minority Views: Jason Ditton, Jon Bannister, Stephen Farrall & Elizabeth Gilchrist`, Scottish Centre for Criminology. (1999) (£5.00)
Summary available: Crime and Criminal Justice Research Findings No.28

The Safer Cities Programme in Scotland – Evaluation of the Aberdeen (North East) Safer Cities Project: MVA. (1999) (£5.00)

Review of National Planning Policy Guidelines: Land Use Consultants. (1999) (£5.00)
Summary available: Development Department Research Findings No.65

Development Department Research Programme 1999-2000. (1999) (Free)

Environment Group Research Programme 1999-2000. (1999) (Free)

Rural Policy Research Programme 1999-2000. (1999) (Free)

Referrals between Advice Agencies and Solicitors: Carole Millar Research. (1999) (£5.00)
Summary available: Legal Studies Research Findings No.21

Life Sentence Prisoners in Scotland: Diane Machin, Nicola Coghill, Liz Levy. (1999) (£3.50)
Summary available: Crime and Criminal Justice Research Findings No.29

Report on a Conference on Domestic Violence in Scotland, Scottish Police College, Tulliallan: The Scottish Office, The Health Education Board for Scotland, The Convention of Scottish Local Authorities, The Scottish Needs Assessment Programme. (1999) (£5.00)

Making it Safe to Speak? Witness Intimidation and Protection in Strathclyde: Nicholas Fyfe, Heather McKay, University of Strathclyde. (1999) (£7.50)

Supporting Court Users: The Pilot In-Court Advice Project in Edinburgh Sheriff Court: Elaine Samuel, Department of Social Policy, University of Edinburgh. (1999) (£5.00)
Summary available: Legal Studies Research Findings No. 22

The Role of Mediation in Family Disputes in Scotland: Jane Lewis, Social and Community Planning Research. (1999) (£5.00)
Summary available: Legal Studies Research Findings No. 23

Research on Women's Issues in Scotland: An Overview: Esther Breitenbach. (1999) (Free)
Summary only available: Women's Issues Research Findings No. 1

Women in Decision-Making in Scotland: A Review of Research: Fiona Myers, University of Edinburgh. (1999) (Free)
Summary only available: Women's Issues Research Findings No. 2

Evaluation of the Debtors (Scotland) Act 1987: Study of Individual Creditors: Debbie Headrick and Alison Platts. (1999) (£5.00)
Summary available: Legal Studies Research Findings No. 10

Evaluation of the Debtors (Scotland) Act 1987: Study of Commercial Creditors: Alison Platts. (1999) (£5.00)
Summary available: Legal Studies Research Findings No. 11

Evaluation of the Debtors (Scotland) Act 1987: Study of Debtors: David Whyte. (1999) (£5.00)
Summary available: Legal Studies Research Findings No. 12

Evaluation of the Debtors (Scotland) Act 1987: Study of Facilitators: Andrew Fleming. (1999) (£5.00)
Summary available: Legal Studies Research Findings No. 13

Evaluation of the Debtors (Scotland) Act 1987: Survey of Poindings and Warrant Sales: Andrew Fleming. (1999) (£5.00)
Summary available: Legal Studies Research Findings No. 14)

Evaluation of the Debtors (Scotland) Act 1987: Survey of Payment Actions in the Sheriff Court: Andrew Fleming, Alison Platts. (1999) (£5.00)
Summary available: Legal Studies Research Findings No. 15

Evaluation of the Debtors (Scotland) Act 1987: Analysis of Diligence Statistics: Andrew Fleming, Alison Platts. (1999) (£5.00)
Summary available: Legal Studies Research Findings No. 16

Evaluation of the Debtors (Scotland) Act 1987: Overview: Alison Platts. (1999) (£5.00)

Looking After Children in Scotland: Susanne Wheelaghan, Malcolm Hill, Moira Borland, Lydia Lambert and John Triseliotis. (1999) (£5.00)
Summary available: Social Work Research Findings No.30

The Evaluation of Childrens Hearings in Scotland: Children in Focus:
Summary available: Social Work Research Findings No.31

Taking Account of Victims in the Criminal Justice System: A Review of the Literature: Andrew Sanders. (1999) (£5.00)
Summary available: Social Work Research Findings No.32

Social Inclusion Bulletin No.1: (1999) (Free)

Geese and their Interactions with Agriculture and the Environment: JS Kirby, M Owen & JM Rowcliffe. (1999) (£10.00)
Summary available: Countryside and Natural Heritage Research Findings No.1

The Recording of Wildlife Crime in Scotland: Ed Conway. (1999) (£10.00)
Summary available: Countryside and Natural Heritage Research Findings No.2

Socio-Economic Benefits from Natura 2000: GF Broom, JR Crabtree, D Roberts & G Hill. (1999) (£5.00)
Summary available: Countryside and Natural Heritage Research Findings No.3

Crime and the Farming Community: The Scottish Farm Crime Survey 1998: Andra Laird, Sue Granville & Ruth Montgomery. (1999) (£10.00)
Summary available: Agricultural Policy Co-ordination and Rural Development Research Findings No.1

New Ideas in Rural Development No 7: Community Development Agents in Rural Scotland: Lynn Watkins & Alison Brown. (1999) (£2.50)
Summary available: Agricultural Policy Co-ordination and Rural Development Research Findings No.2

New Ideas in Rural Development No 8: Tackling Crime in Rural Scotland: Mary-Ann Smyth. (1999) (£2.50)
Summary available: Agricultural Policy Co-ordination and Rural Development Research Findings No.3

Study of the Impact of Migration in Rural Scotland: Professor Allan Findlay, Dr David Short, Dr Aileen Stockdale, Anne Findlay, Lin N Li, Lorna Philip. (1999) (£10.00)
Summary available: Agricultural Policy Co-ordination and Rural Development Research Findings No.4

An Electoral System for Scottish Local Government: Modelling Some Alternatives: John Curtice. (1999) (£5.00)

Writing for the CRU Research Series: Ann Millar, Sue Morris & Alison Platts. (1999) (Free)

The Effect of Closed Circuit Television on Recorded Crime Rates and Public Concern about Crime in Glasgow: Jason Ditton, Emma Short, Samuel Phillips, Clive Norris & Gary Armstrong. (1999) (£5.00)
Summary available: Crime and Criminal Justice Research Findings No.30

Working with Persistent Juvenile Offenders: An Evaluation of the Apex CueTen Project: David Lobley & David Smith. (1999) (£5.00)
Summary available: Crime and Criminal Justice Research Findings No.31

The Role and Effectiveness of Community Councils with Regard to Community Consultation: Robina Goodlad, John Flint, Ade Kearns, Margaret Keoghan, Ronan Paddison & Mike Raco. (1999) (£5.00)

Perceptions of Local Government: A Report of Focus Group Research: Carole Millar Research. (1999) (£5.00)

Supporting Parenting in Scotland: Sheila Henderson. (1999) (£5.00)
Summary available: Social Work Research Findings No.33

Investigation of Knife Stab Characteristics: I. Biomechanics of Knife Stab Attacks; II. Development of Body Tissue Simulant: Bioengineering Unit & Department of Mechanical Engineering, University of Strathclyde. (1999) (£5.00)

City-Wide Urban Regeneration: Lessons from Good Practice: Professor Michael Carley & Karryn Kirk, School of Planning & Housing, Heriot-Watt University. (1999) (£5.00)
Summary available: Development Department Research Findings No.66

An Examination of Unsuccessful Priority Partnership Area Bids: Peter Taylor, Ivan Turok & Annette Hastings, Department of Urban Studies, University of Glasgow. (1999) (£5.00)
Summary available: Development Department Research Findings No.67

The Community Impact of Traffic Calming Schemes: Ross Silcock Ltd, Social Research Associates. (1999) (£10.00)
Summary available: Development Department Research Findings No.68

The People's Panel in Scotland: Wave 1 (June-September 1998): Dr Nuala Gormley. (1999) (Free)
Summary only available: General Research Findings No.1

The People's Panel in Scotland: Wave 2 (August-November 1998): Dr Nuala Gormley. (1999) (Free)
Summary only available: General Research Findings No.2

Evaluation of Prevention of Environmental Pollution from Agricultural Activity (PEPFAA) Code: Peter Evans, Market Research Scotland. (1999) (£5.00)
Summary available: General Research Findings No.3

Evaluation of Prevention of Environmental Pollution from Agricultural Activity (PEPFAA) Code: Peter Evans, Market Research Scotland. (1999) (£5.00)
Summary available: General Research Findings No.3

Review of Safer Routes to School in Scotland: Derek Halden Consultancy in association with David McGuigan. (1999) (£5.00)

Climate Change: Scottish Implications Scoping Study: Andrew Kerr & Simon Allen, University of Edinburgh; Simon Shackley, UMIST; Ronnie Milne, Institute of Terrestrial Ecology. (1999) (£5.00)
Summary available: Environment Group Research Findings No.5

City-Wide Urban Regeneration: Lessons from Good Practice: Professor Michael Carley & Karryn Kirk. (1999) (£5.00
Summary available: Development Department Research Findings No.66

An Examination of Unsuccessful Priority Partnership Area Bids: Peter Taylor, Ivan Turok & Annette Hastings. (1999) (£5.00)
Summary available: Development Department Research Findings No.67

The Children's Traffic Club in Scotland: Katie Bryan-Brown & Gordon Harland. (1999) (£5.00)
Summary available: Development Department Research Findings No.69

An Evaluation of the New Life for Urban Scotland Initiative in Castlemilk, Ferguslie Park, Wester Hailes and Whitfield: Cambridge Policy Consultants. (1999) (£10.00)
Summary available: Development Department Research Findings No.70

National Monitoring and Interim Evaluation of the Rough Sleepers Initiative in Scotland: Anne Yanetta & Hilary Third (School of Planning & Housing, ECA/Heriot-Watt University) & Isobel Anderson (HPPU, University of Stirling). (1999) (£5.00)
Summary available: Development Department Research Findings No.71

Social Inclusion Research Bulletin No.2. (1999) (Free)

Costs in the Planning Service: Paula Gilder Consulting. (1999) (£5.00
Summary available: Development Department Research Findings No.72

Evaluation of the Teenwise Alcohol Projects: Simon Anderson & Beckie Sawyer. (1999) (£6.00)
Summary available: Crime and Criminal Justice Research Findings No.34

The Work of Precognition Agents in Criminal Cases: David J Christie & Susan R Moody (University of Dundee). (1999) (£5.00)
Summary available: Crime and Criminal Justice Research Findings No.32

Counting the Cost: Crime Against Business in Scotland: John Burrows, Simon Anderson, Joshua Bamfield, Matt Hopkins & Dave Ingram. (1999) (£10.00)
Summary available: Crime and Criminal Justice Research Findings No.35

Park and Ride in Scotland: Transport Research Laboratory and Strathclyde Passenger Transport. (1999) (£5.00)
Summary available: Development Department Research Findings No.74

Understanding Offending Among Young People: Janet Jamieson, Gill McIvor & Cathy Murray. (1999) (£16.00)
Summary available: Social Work Research Findings No.37

The View from Arthur's Seat: A Literature Review of Housing and Support Options 'Beyond Scotland': Ken Simons & Debbie Watson (Norah Fry Research Centre, University of Bristol). (1999) (£5.00)

"If You Don't Ask You Don't Get": Review of Services to People with Learning Disabilities: The Views of People who use Services and their Carers: Kirsten Stalker, Liz Cadogan, Margaret Petrie, Chris Jones, Jill Murray (Scottish Human Services). (1999) (£5.00)

Further information on any of the above is available by contacting:

Dr C P A Levein
Chief Research Officer
The Scottish Office Central Research Unit
Room J1-5
Saughton House
Broomhouse Drive
Edinburgh
EH11 3XA

or by accessing the World Wide Website: www.scotland.gov.uk